WORDS TO THE WORDLESS

LIVING LEGACY OF SWAMI CHINMAYANANDA

Published by
Chinmaya Mission West
P.O. Box 129, Piercy, CA 95587 U.S.A.
Tel: (707) 247-3488
Email: publications@chinmayamission.org
Website: www.chinmayamission.org

Deep gratitude and reverent obeisance to Pūjya Swami Tejomayananda for his loving guidance, continual support, and invaluable inputs.

Special thanks to Brni. Prarthana Chaitanya, who provided access to all the material in Chinmaya Archives, especially the precious letters of Pūjya Gurudev.

Grateful acknowledgment to Swamini Vimalananda, Swamini Nishchalananda, Ācārya Atma Chaitanya, Swami Sridharananda, Swami Ramatmananda, Ācārya Varsha, Manju Tyagi, Anjali Singh, Lakshmi Reddy, Vijaya Saradhi and Ramachandra Murti for their inputs about regional publications. Heartfelt thanks to Bharati Sukhatankar, who shared her experiences of writing and editing for Pūjya Gurudev. Special thanks to Isabel Taylor, Rudite Emir, Ācārya Vilasini, Jorge-Luis Jauregui, Swami Siddhananda, Asha Kamdar, Yuva Veer M. Santosh, and Br. Saket Chaitanya for their contribution. Many thanks to Cauvery Bhalla, Vaishali Lokhande and the other staff of Chinmaya Archives, K. C. Patnaik, Subhashree Raghav and Shamika and the design team of Chinmaya Kalpanam for their timely help.

Editorial Support by the Mananam Team
Margaret Dukes, David Dukes, Neena Dev, Rudite Emir, Br. Eric, Rashmi Mehrotra, Arun Mehrotra, Padmashree Rao, and Aarthi Ramalingam

Author
Smt. Parvathy Raman

Design and Layout
Mot Juste Communication Services Private Limited, Chennai 600 018

Printed by
Silverpoint Press Pvt. Ltd., Mumbai, India

Library of Congress Control Number: 2015953362
ISBN: 978-1-60827-016-3

The **mananam** Series

CHINMAYA BIRTH CENTENARY CELEBRATION SERIES

WORDS TO THE WORDLESS

LIVING LEGACY OF SWAMI CHINMAYANANDA

CHINMAYA PUBLICATIONS

CHINMAYA MISSION WEST PUBLICATIONS DIVISION

Contents

Foreword

In today's world of modern technology, information is available in many forms. And yet, the printed word has a special place. Whether it be a flight manual or a railway timetable, an itinerary or a telephone book, a recipe or a road map, the printed version is still sought after. One of my tech-savvy friends found out one day that his complete schedule of appointments and his entire list of business contacts were deleted, because something went wrong with his computer. Now he makes it a point to have a printed copy on hand.

Books can be read even in digital version using e-readers. Whatever may be the equipment used to read them, the power of the written word cannot be denied. And, of course, printed books have their own special charm. The touch and feel of a book still has its unique attraction.

Study of any subject depends on books. Physics or chemistry, archaeology or fashion design, we find innumerable books that enable new areas of study. We need books at our jñāna yajñas and spiritual camps also; we cannot proceed with a study of the scriptures without the relevant texts in hand. Pūjya Gurudev insisted that everyone should have a copy of the *Bhagavad-gītā* and should try chanting the verses studied during the discourses. Study Groups have their own syllabus based on a graded set of selected books.

Books are our companions on the spiritual path. When we listen to lectures, we feel very inspired. But the effect of mere listening does not last very long. When the same topic is presented in the form of a book, we can read it whenever we want, and at our own pace. Sometimes we may read a single line which opens up a new line of thought, and we may want to think about it before we proceed further.

This reminds me of an incident with Pūjya Gurudev. I had composed some verses and, as usual, I gave my composition to Gurudev to read. After some days, when he did not mention anything about it, I brought up the topic and asked if he had read it. "Not yet," he replied. In those days he had some trouble with his eyes; so I requested him not to strain himself and offered to read the work to him. He gently shook his head and said, "I like to read it slowly, so that I can pause and think." I was taken aback that Gurudev said such a thing about my humble effort at writing. How much more earnest thinking and reflection should go into our reading of spiritual texts!

Books are wonderful gifts for all occasions. Whether they are for children, friends, elders, or even strangers, books make appropriate gifts. And sometimes a book can mark the turning point in your life. A word or a sentence can have a major impact and trigger a new direction in your life. I remember reading a small booklet of Swami Vivekananda's writings, which influenced me very strongly in my youth. Ācārya Vinoba Bhave, another inspiring personality, recalls that when he was a child, his father came home one day with a gift that he called 'imperishable.' The boy thought it must be an unbreakable toy. But it turned out to be the *Bhagavad-gītā*. He did not know then that his whole life would be guided by the *Gītā* and that he would later write a commentary on it.

Today, we are able to study the scriptures because they were written down in the form of books. Earlier they were handed down orally (śruti). The great sage Bhagavān Veda Vyāsa compiled the knowledge available in the oral tradition and codified it in the form of the four Vedas. Later, Ādi Śaṅkarācārya wrote commentaries on the Vedas, which are very precious to us, because without them it is difficult to comprehend what is said in the Upaniṣads.

In Hindu culture, we worship books as a form of Mother Sarasvatī, the goddess of learning. When we approach the scriptural texts with love and reverence, they reveal their deepest meanings to us.

Books serve to propagate very effectively the knowledge in any field. Knowing this, Pūjya Gurudev encouraged Chinmaya Mission's publication division from its initial stages. Now, in the twenty-first century, we are lucky to have a rich collection of reading material. Many people who never met Pūjya Gurudev Swami Chinmayananda or Parama Guru Swami Tapovan Maharaj are able to read their books and learn in depth. For example, when reading travelogues like *Wanderings in the Himalayas* and *My Trek through Uttarkhand*, we can walk along with the authors even today and see the world through their eyes. Chinmaya Publications also produces cassettes, CDs, and DVDs, which serve the same purpose as the printed books to impart the message of Vedānta. Of late, we have begun to webcast programs, live or recorded, through the Chinmaya Channel. All such efforts help us to stay connected and sustain our inspiration to continue on the spiritual path.

I am very happy that this volume on the work of our publications division is being published as part of the Chinmaya Birth Centenary Celebration Series. This book will give a comprehensive idea about the origin, growth, present scope, and future possibilities of Chinmaya Publications.

With Prem & Om,

Swami Tejomayananda   October 15, 2015
Head, Chinmaya Mission Worldwide   Mumbai

Introduction

Pūjya Guruji Swami Tejomayananda, while teaching the Dakṣiṇāmūrti Stotram to the brahmacārīs of the Vedānta Course, pointed out: "We may admire the power of silence, but never underestimate the power of the word. All teaching has to begin with words." His words echoed his Guru Swami Chinmayananda's powerful statement that puts the process of spiritual growth in a nutshell: "From Words to the Wordless, and so Worldless." This crisp phrase indicates the entire process of listening to the words of the teaching; reading and reflecting on what has been heard; and immersing oneself in the silence that arises when the teaching is internalized — what the scriptures term as śravaṇa, manana, and nididhyāsana. Where the words end, the world ends, too, for one reaches the realm beyond words.

Indeed, where would we be without the powerful call of our Pūjya Gurudev, who spent his lifetime discoursing upon the Gītā and the Upaniṣads? Gurudev would invariably follow up the evening lectures bristling with dynamic spiritual energy, with the unforgettable morning meditation sessions that brought us to the still center of our being.

His words continue to ring in our ears and echo in our hearts. Mother Sarasvatī danced on his tongue, flowing out in powerful oratory, bringing forth the rich meanings and the innumerable subtle nuances embedded in the scriptures of Vedānta. His irrefutable logic was laced with examples from everyday life, which resonated powerfully with his listeners. Oh yes, the words were stinging at times, whipping up the listeners from their spiritual slumber; while, at other times, they tickled the listeners to laugh at their own follies.

Pūjya Gurudev was fully aware of the power of the word to reach out through the corridors of time to the future generations of seekers who may never see him in person. In his own time, he reached out through the printed word to people across the world. He left behind a legacy of many volumes of books and recorded talks that inspire people even today.

This book is an attempt to look at his legacy of words that takes us, if not to the *world*-less, at least to a *word*-less state of wonder.

Note: The image of the tree, with its roots, trunk, and branches, is used to bring out the genesis, structure, and development of the publication division of Chinmaya Mission. It does not, in any way, reflect on the relative importance or value of the scriptural texts.

Pūjya Gurudev Swami Chinmayananda was known as 'Swamiji' in the earlier years. It was only later that many other Swamis were initiated in Chinmaya Mission, and he began to be addressed as 'Gurudev,' especially so after his Mahāsamādhi. The old devotees still use the word 'Swamiji' to refer to him in their reminiscences. Hence, to maintain authenticity, we refer to him as 'Swamiji' in the earlier parts of this book.

PART ONE

THE ROOTS

॥ॐ॥

The Roots

Swami Tapovanam:
Words That Nourished Chinmaya

One of the images cherished by Chinmaya Mission members is that of Śrī Swami Tapovanam, Gurudev Swami Chinmayananda's Guru, sitting in silence on the veranda of his simple hut in Uttarkashi. Behind this supreme serenity was the deep understanding of the mystic words of the vast scriptures of Vedānta.

Swami Chinmayananda seated at the feet of his Guru, Swami Tapovan Maharaj, at Uttarkashi

For many years, he taught learned scholars, in both Rishikesh and Uttarkashi, unraveling knotty phrases and ambiguous words with his unfailing logic and clarity of expression. Noisy paṇḍits, fond of hair-splitting arguments, were stilled into silence by this scriptural stalwart.

Few know that Swami Tapovanam was, in his youth, a brilliant orator. His speeches were so commanding that there was a constant demand for him to talk at various platforms — schools and colleges, literary clubs, and public meetings. His keen intellect enabled him to speak fluently on a variety of subjects — social reform, literature, religion, and culture. Though he was well-versed in English, his chosen medium of communication was his native tongue — Malayalam.

When Palakkad welcomed illustrious personalities like Mahātmā Gandhi or Rabindranath Tagore at massive gatherings, it was through the voice of Subramania, or Chippu Kutty Nair, as Swamiji was known at that time. His eloquence was such that one of the listeners wrote to him, "I very much wish I could become your disciple in the art of public speaking. Kindly accept me as your pupil and give all necessary tips."[1]

It was around this time (1916) that he published a magazine named after Gopala Krishna Gokhale, the great social reformer and nationalist leader, who had recently passed away, leaving a blazing trail in the struggle for India's independence. However, as editor of the magazine, Subramania scrupulously avoided articles about political issues and concentrated on writing about social reform, morality, and religion.

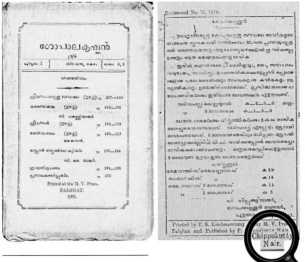

◄ *Scan of front and back page of Gopalakrishna magazine with the publisher's name, P. Chippukutty Nair, on the back*

---

[1] *Īśvara Darśanam*, chapter 7

Within a few years, he realized that this kind of service for mankind, which he had undertaken, also led him to associate with people who hankered after fame and glory. Understanding the futility of such play with words for a person whose goal was to reach beyond the world of words, he gave up public speaking and journalism altogether.

From his early years, Swami Tapovanam showed a strong inclination for spiritual life and he also had a literary bent of mind. At the age of eighteen, he wrote a poem called 'Vibhākaram,' and he also used to contribute regularly to many literary journals. He was barely twenty-one years old when he lost his father. His mind sought solace in composing a devotional poem titled 'Viṣṇu Yamakam.' This was a devotional poem in Malayalam, published in 1912 by Bharat Vilas Press of Triśivaperūr (Thrissur) and was hailed as a rare gem by the literary community of those times. Though all his biographies mention this poem, it remained unavailable to Chinmaya Mission members for many years, until Brni. Prarthana Chaitanya unearthed it a century later, on Tapovan Jayanti Day 2011, in an ancient library in Kerala — Appan Tampurān Smārakam.

▲ *The front cover and first page of* Viṣṇu Yamakam

In 1923, Swamiji left home to lead a wandering monk's life in the Himalayas. A record of his discovery of divine joy among the lofty mountain ranges is to be found in *Himagiri Vihāram*, written in Malayalam and published serially in *Sāhitya Pariṣad Traimāsikam*, a quarterly magazine in Malayalam. This was later translated and published under the title *Wanderings in the Himalayas*.

The years that followed saw many rare and valuable treatises flow from his pen — commentaries in Malayalam on *Īśāvāsya Upaniṣad*, *Kenopaniṣad*, *Kaṭhopaniṣad*, and *Śāṇḍilya Bhakti Sūtra*, none of which were published or are available today. However, a rare copy of his travelogue *Kailāsa Yātrā*, describing in detail his two visits to Mount Kailas, was found and translated from Malayalam into English by Swamini Niranjanananda.

While residing in Uttarkashi and Gangotri, he composed *Saumya Kāśīśa Stotram* (1930),[2] *Gaumukhī Yātrā* (1937), *Gangottarī Kṣetra Māhātmyam* (1937), *Śrī Gangā Stotram* (1940), and the autobiographical work *Īśvara Darśanam* (1947–48) — all of them written in Sanskrit and most of them published by Pandit Vallabharam Sharma, an ardent admirer and devotee of Swami Tapovan Maharaj. *Badarīśa Stotram* was written in 1933 during his visit to Badrinath. Śrī Vasudevan Namboodiri, the then main priest (Rawal) of the temple, found it to be a treasure, and with Swamiji's permission got it printed, with a Hindi commentary, by Venkateswara Press in Mumbai, fully sponsored by the Badrinath Temple.

▲ *Pandit Vallabharam Sharma*

---

2   All the years mentioned in parenthesis are the years of the first publication.

▲ *Swami Mahadeva Vanam*

Īśvara Darśanam, highly acclaimed by scholars, was translated into Malayalam by Swami Mridananda of Ramakrishna Mission, and then into English by Śrī T. N. Kesava Pillai. The initial chapters of this English translation were appreciated and endorsed by Śrī Swami Tapovan Maharaj in his own lifetime. Perumbavoor Krishna Pillai, later known as Swami Mahadeva Vanam, played a major role in preserving and publishing Swami Tapovanam's books in the early years.

Sri Swami Mahadeva Vanam, a very great devotee of Sri Gurudev Tapovanam and who has been publishing all Sri Tapovan Maharaj's works at Sri Gurudev's (Swami Tapovanam's) own command, is now here. It has been decided now that the Chinmaya Publication Trust (Madras) will take over all Sri Gurudev's books and publish them under a separate series, Tapovan Granthavali. This was one of Sri Gurudev's parting written instructions. Chinmaya and Mahadeva Vanam will fulfill it now. Sri Gurudev's autobiographical work, a fluent volume on Vedanta, *Ishvara Darshanam*, has been translated into Malayalam and is being printed. Its English version is now with the translator, Sri Kesava Pillai, who had earlier translated *Wanderings in the Himalayas*. We expect that Sri Pillai, though in bed these days, will complete the job in another month or two.

– Report from Sandeepany Sadhanalaya,
published in *Tapovan Prasad*, July 1968

Later on, all those books were published with commentaries and translations in English by the publication division of Chinmaya Mission. Some of the commentaries were written by Pūjya Gurudev Swami Chinmayananda, and one can see how deeply he had studied them. Swami Tapovanam's words nourished his beloved Chinmaya, both in their written form, in which the essence of the scriptures was ensconced, and in the spoken medium, during the personal one-on-one teachings on the sanctified veranda of Tapovan Kuti, with the gentle murmuring of the holy river Bhagirathi in the background providing the 'Om' that filled the silence between the words.

Swami Sivananda: Words That Sang and Danced

Swami Sivananda was a staunch missionary, determined to reach the maximum number of people with the message of the scriptures. Healthy and well-built, his very physical frame exuding good cheer

and strength, he roared from the banks of Mother Ganga at Rishikesh, exhorting all who could hear, to understand their essential nature as immortal Bliss. His songs, in simple English, bursting with energy, swept the listeners along into a divine mood. His words sanctified people, as much as the holy waters of the gushing river did. Little wonder that Chinmaya, the skeptical journalist, was transformed into a relentless seeker under his influence.

▲ *Swami Sivananda*

Knowing the power of words to transform people, Swami Sivananda made full use of the English language to reach people who otherwise would never have understood the scholarly wisdom couched in Sanskrit. He was a prolific writer and wrote many books, as well as small booklets for free distribution. His inexhaustible zeal and energy sprang from the inner fount of silence, where he had drunk his fill.

A doctor by profession, Swami Sivananda matched his words with silent service to the humble and needy. He would provide not only medicine, but also food, and quite often would personally nurse the patients back to health, propping up their morale with spiritual talk all the while. Sustaining himself with dry *roṭīs*, and following a very austere way of life, he would distribute whatever food he had to nourish the sick. A steady stream of patients would flow into the charitable dispensary that he had set up.

In many ways, Swami Chinmayananda found a role model in Swami Sivananda. He imbibed the missionary spirit from this Master, who had sparked off the divine quest in him, and who had bestowed the ochre robes in which he shone the rest of his life. Following in his footsteps, Chinmaya also thundered in English from many platforms, but took the journey much farther, traveling far and wide across the globe to reach people who otherwise would not have ever heard of the *Bhagavad-gītā* or the Upaniṣads. Like his Master, Swami Chinmayananda also wrote innumerable letters, keeping in touch with devotees all over the world, encouraging and inspiring them on the spiritual path. He combined the quest for spiritual knowledge with social service, especially in the field of education.

The words of the two spiritual giants, Swami Sivananda and Swami Tapovanam, who also were the best of friends, nurtured Swami Chinmayananda through his early years, so that he could discover the silent Source of all words, revel in It, and then drench the world in a shower of words that could wash away spiritual ignorance.

▲ *Swami Sivananda and Swami Tapovanam*

Journalistic Background: The Art of Weaving Words

The young Balakrishna Menon, who was destined to become Swami Chinmayananda later, was groomed in language and literature in Lucknow University. He enrolled himself there to study English literature along with law and obtain a master's degree. He must have enjoyed the course, and the impact on him was evident even in the early 1950s, when he would quote Wordsworth and the other English poets with great felicity and ease, both in his talks and his writings.

One instance of his masterly use of literary studies during his later years as a spiritual teacher is his clever adaptation of Plato's myth of the cave in describing the relationship of the Guru and śiṣya, which was in essence the story of his own struggle as a spiritual teacher.

The Myth of the Cave

Once upon a time, there was a cave in which a lot of people lived. There was a huge roaring fire, and the people lived and moved by the light of this fire. They knew nothing of the world outside the cave. They believed firmly that theirs was the only world there was. They lived among the shadows, ate, slept, and fought in the confines of this cave.

A man there was who dared to walk away from the crowd. He walked away from the fire, the only light known to him, into the darkness beyond. He stumbled in the dark, hurt himself in many ways, stepped on jagged stones, bumped into rocks, and yet walked on. Long and dreary was the journey, but by and by, he saw light. The light became brighter and brighter, and finally he emerged out of the cave.

▶

He saw the green trees, the gurgling streams, the blue sky, the floating white clouds, all beautiful beyond compare. Never had he dreamed that such a wonderful world existed — bright, sunny, and colorful. His heart was flooded with joy. He rolled on the grass, felt the soft flowers, danced and sang, reveled in this newly discovered world, for a long, long time.

Slowly, he sat up. He remembered his kinsmen in the cave. He had to bring them out to share this joyous new world. He walked back into the cave.

He saw them around the fire, busy in their own world. He tried to tell them what he had seen. They were too busy to hear what he said. Some who heard, laughed at him, jeered and ridiculed him. Others condemned him for walking away from the fire, all alone.

He bided his time patiently, watchfully, waiting to see one who was likely to give him a hearing, someone no more enamored by life among the shadows. Such a one he found; he talked to him and convinced him to walk away from the fire, beyond the darkness. "I shall walk ahead; just follow me," he said, and walked along, reassuring his follower as the darkness enveloped them slowly. "Step this way; avoid the jutting rock," he continued giving instructions. The darkness thickened. Suddenly he felt that there was nobody following him. He turned around and, indeed, the follower had fled back to the familiar fire in the cave.

He was disappointed, but he was not the one to give up so easily. He walked back again into the cave and looked patiently for the right person. This time, when he found such a one, he was very careful. Being wiser than before, he asked him to walk

▶

ahead, himself following behind, with instructions. There was no way the man could escape. It grew darker, but he comforted and reassured him, guiding him gently and telling him that the light was not far away. Soon enough, it became less dark, and slowly they emerged into the sunlight. He saw his companion get out of the cave, eyes shining with joy, running, shouting, and rolling on the grass. A smile of satisfaction hovered around his face ...

– Swami Chinmayananda

By the time he finished the course in literature, Balakrishna Menon was intensely involved in the Indian freedom movement. He had much to write about, and the best career option was that of a journalist. His initial efforts as a freelancer were a dismal failure. Here is an excerpt from an amusing description about his journalistic efforts, which was a part of an article by him published in *The Indian Journalist* in 1946:

Out from the college desks, with a puffed-up head held erect over a swollen heart bleeding with pride at my degree, I decided to make a career of journalism. I knocked at the door-panes of a few of the Bombay editors' sanctums. All I learned there was that the editors respect previous experience more than degrees. I was willing to earn experience if they would but allow me, but they simply won't!!! And so I planned to make a gatecrash entry into this guarded preserve of mediocre writers. My plan was simple, so simple that it did not work!

Reaching my room, I dashed off some four articles on the social injustices of our country, in orthodox Addisonian style, with plenty of quotations from Milton, Shakespeare, Swift, and

Goldsmith! These were dispatched to different editors in a couple of days. With tiring impatience, I waited and watched the issues daily. After a week, all of them were returned to me with the respective editor's regret and compliment slip. I cursed the dull-headedness of the day's editors and their inability to recognize the merits of a worthy article when they see one!

All his experiences were grist for the mill; he would turn them all into articles. The agony of trying to get a sub-editor's job is also narrated with self-deprecating humor in another article in the same magazine in September 1946:

Shaking in all my limbs in excitement, I entered the editor's room. With a clattering heart alternately bubbling with happiness and tumbling in disastrous fears, slowly, almost stealthily, I reached an overburdened table. As I approached, I could see only the shapely head of the grey-haired editor sitting bent at his work. With a sensitive quick movement of the hand, he showed me a chair on his right. His eyes were thoughtful and preoccupied. His physical body seemed to recognize my presence, but his spirits were still far away, reveling in a world of its own thoughts.

I watched his oily, pock-marked, ruddy face and wondered at his age and at his exclusive thoughts. He jerked his shoulders and pushed aside his work. With a laborious effort, as it were, the short little body, sitting doubled up in a revolving chair, turned toward me.

All the while, torn with fear of refusal, failure, and disappointment, I sat on the uncomfortable, stiff chair, twisting and turning my fingers. It should not have surprised me at all, if somebody had told me then that during the interview I had been biting my nails! I had no choice but to submit myself to the searching scrutiny of a pair of small little eyes. I have yet to see another pair as shy and weak as his and yet withal so piercing and grave.

Breaking abruptly the growing silence of the room, he said, "So, you want to be a sub-editor, eh? Well, I think I will take you up on it, but you must be ready to work day or night, fourteen to twenty hours a day … and that, too, sometimes at a stretch. And you must learn typewriting in the next three months. These are my conditions. On my part, I shall try to make a 'sub' of you."

In all earnest gratitude and honest sincerity, I accepted his terms and promised to work always as best as I could, and I shook hands with my guru and guide, Mr. K. Rama Rao, who has been rightly acclaimed as the greatest sub-editor in Indian journalism.

Little did I realize that every phrase in Mr. Rama Rao's innocent-looking speech was to come true. When I reached my hotel that day, I said to myself, "No, it can never be. It is just an exaggeration. Fourteen to twenty hours a day! We are too civilized for that today and the age of slavery is dead long ago." But my experience tells me that every word of it was true; my later studies in the literature of journalism convinces me that Mr. Rama Rao had anxiously tried to put the total demands as leniently as possible.

One who is earnest in entering journalism in its editorial side should at the very outset learn each day to forget the hour of his arrival at the office. I should not say that he must ignore the clock; in no other profession does the clock form such an important integral part. 'Tick-tick' swings the pendulum. The minute hand moves in impatient hurry. The dial grins in awful glee. It is a severe reminder, a perpetual threat and a never-ending challenge to a sub-editor. There are a thousand and one things to be done, and all within the scheduled time. No 'dak' [post] can wait even a moment after its immutable hour.

▲ *P. B. K. Menon*

The young P. B. K. Menon landed a job with the *National Herald* and worked there from December 1945 to February 1947. Many of the articles written then have been published in the *Tapovan Prasad* magazine.[3] They give us an interesting insight into his life at that stage and show his keen observation, innate sense of humor, and mastery over the English language.

As a part of the newspaper industry, P. B. K. Menon was trained in the intricacies of the entire process of printing and publishing — the careful editing, the meticulous proofreading, the tedious typesetting, the art of block-making, the choice of paper, the techniques of printing, and the intricacies of marketing. Those were the days before the advent of computers; today, it is difficult for us to even imagine a life without soft copies and digital printing.

Yagna Prasad: Spoken Word to Written Word

The journalistic background was a big asset for Swami Chinmayananda when he entered the spiritual field. The printing and dissemination of spiritual literature was an integral part of the yajña scheme as he

---

[3] The internationally distributed monthly magazine of Chinmaya Mission

envisioned it. This is clear from his letter dated October 15, 1951, to Śrī
Madhava Menon:

This winter (Jan–March), Chinmaya is to go to Poona to act as the
Chief Priest in a 100 days' Upanishad Gyana Yagna, which they are
organizing there as per instructions from here. This rather unorthodox
yagna has nothing to do much with the vast burning away of ghee and
food grains. It is a Jnana Yagna consisting mainly of three items:

1. Daily morning classes — to teach Kena and Katha Upanishad with
   Sri Sankara Bhashya to fit aspirants only.

2. Daily evening satsang — discourses upon the mantras in the above Upanishads — open to all — even to Christians, Muslims, Buddhists or Jains.

3. Reports of the above i.e. the class notes and the discourses to be edited and published each week for free distribution in India and abroad.

This is the main part of the Jnana Yagna. Naturally, greater the number printed each week and effectively circulated, greater the success. But neither the printing charge nor postage is cheap these days! The yagna depends entirely upon the patronage of bhaktas. Won't you bring thy offerings to this great effort for the dissemination of the sacred Truths contained in the Religion of Vedanta?

▲ *Swamiji at work compiling* Yagna Prasad *booklets*

Hence, from the very beginning, his talks were compiled into books to spread the message of the scriptures to an increasing number of readers. The books were also an essential link for the devotees to remember what they had heard, giving them time to assimilate the ideas. Further, textbooks were needed so that devotees could refer to the ślokas, chant along, and get the maximum benefit from his lectures. And in those days, it was not easy to come by texts of the Upaniṣads, and certainly not with commentary in English. With a detailed knowledge of the world of printing and publishing, Swamiji could efficiently guide the devotees through the entire process, avoiding common pitfalls.

CHINMAYA'S WORK IS
DEDICATED

TO

THE SRUTIES
THAT TOLD ME WHAT REALITY IS

TO

SREE SWAMI TAPOVANJI MAHARAJ
(*of Uttarkashi*)

WHO

GUIDED ME TO THE END AND PUSHED ME
INTO THE BEYOND

AND

TO

Sad Guru Dev
SREE SWAMI SIVANANDAJI MAHARAJ
(*of Rishikesh*)

WHO

SHOWED ME IN HIS LIFE HOW TO
LIVE AND ACT

IN GOD AS GOD ! !

▲ *Dedication page in the first* Yagna Prasad *booklet*

Swamiji had the foresight to arrange for the devotees to record his talks in shorthand from the very first yajña in Pune. The notes thus recorded were collected every three or four days and compiled into booklets under his direct supervision. Titled *Yagna Prasad*, these booklets carried the picture of a lighted torch held aloft on the front cover. By 1954, when Sheela Sharma began to translate some of them into Hindi, Swamiji gave her strict instructions:

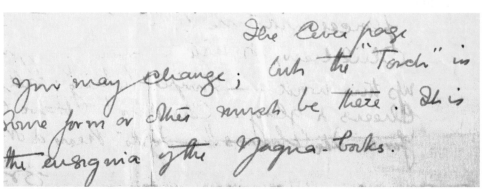

The cover page you may change, but the "Torch" in some form or the other must be there. It is the insignia of the Yagna books.

During the period of the Yagna in Palakkad (January 7–27, 1954), after the lectures were over, Swamiji used to dictate to me the texts taken on that day to publish in the weekly *Yagna Prasad Bulletin*. Swamiji and I used to sit up until 12 o'clock in the night to complete this work. We were moving as closely as brothers for exchanging our ideas and clearing doubts. We shared food with each other and slept in the same room.

– Br. Radhakrishnan
(later Swami Jyotirmayananda)

The *Yagna Prasad* was distributed freely to those who attended the yajña discourses. With great efficiency and forethought, Swamiji built up contact with his devotees by collecting their addresses, and as he moved on to the venue of the next *yajña*, he kept posting the new issues of *Yagna Prasad* to them, thus keeping them inspired on the path. Further, new readers who chanced upon the *Yagna Prasad* and flipped through the pages, found their interest in the subject kindled to such an extent that sooner or later they landed up in the yajñaśālā, the venue of the discourses. The impact of the *Yagna Prasad* can be gauged by the feedback given by some of the devotees.

The *Yagna Prasad* booklets first reached us during Swamiji's second Yagna conducted at Madras in April 1, 1953. I was rather empty-headed then, nothing but the shallow product of an Anglicized school. The very word 'Yagna' and the picture of a lighted torch on the front cover paper brought before my mind the vision of a ritualistic havan with tufted brahmin priests presiding, looking woefully out of date. And my mind shied away from the scene. So the *Yagna Prasads* remained on a costly table until someone buried them in the bookshelf among old magazines. Thus, I wantonly threw away the precious jewel of Truth, which would have enriched my mind beyond measure.

Life continued as of old, and it was one frantic search for happiness in the centres of gaiety — picture-houses, glittering shops, the club, and so on. Meanwhile, the *Yagna Prasads* continued to come from Madura, Coimbatore, and Delhi — nobody knew who was sending them or why they were sent. And then, one day, one of my brothers chanced to read one and was instantly struck with the profound wisdom it contained. He recommended it to the rest of us, and as all of us brothers and sisters have the same taste in books and most other things, a germ of interest was kindled in the Yagna. It rapidly grew to all-absorbing proportions, and I began looking forward eagerly to each *Yagna Prasad*. Swamiji, at the time, was lecturing on the *Kathopanishad* in Delhi. I visualized it as a sort of intellectual treat, and the news that Swamiji was coming to Madras for his second Yagna in that city filled me with the liveliest anticipation.

Smt. Radha Kurup
(Kozhikode, 1957, *Hail Renaissance*, Volume 1)

A blessed relative of mine used to get the *Yagna Prasad* packets from His Holiness Swami Chinmayanandaji in those days, but being a very busy lawyer, he was not making full use of them. He passed them on to me. Like most other people, I was merely a God-fearing man until then, with material prosperity as the goal of my life.

When I started studying the *Yagna Prasad* booklets, I was not only inspired to the roots of my hair, but I developed an irresistible thirst to have darshan of the great philosopher who distributed the *Yagna Prasad*. At a satsang in Delhi, the program of His Holiness Swami Chinmayanandaji was announced: *Kenopanishad* at Kashmere Gate! *Vivekachoodamani* at Karol Bagh!

By studying the *Yagna Prasad*, I was convinced that I belonged to the class of 'college educated illiterates,' and so I availed myself of the opportunity to attend *Kenopanishad* at the Delhi University. Swamiji entered the Convocation Hall precisely at the appointed time. With three "*Om, Om, Om,*" Swamiji began talking …

– O. K. Balakrishnan Nambiar

(Bombay, 1960, *Hail Renaissance*, Volume 2)

Much later, at the end of the 25th Jñāna Yajña, in an article that was published in the souvenir *Hail Renaissance*, Volume 1, Swami Chinmayananda recalled this initial process of publishing *Yagna Prasad* booklets and how it led to the first journal, *Tyagi*, which remains a landmark in the Chinmaya movement:

The Yagnas keep slowly developing under the pressure of new experiences. Thus, recently, we have achieved in it the idea of printing the selected chapters of the *Geeta*, or the very mantras of the Upanishads, in handy pocket booklets, so that all seekers may have the textbook in hand during the discourses. I started collecting the addresses of all those who attended, along with their "Voluntary Guru Dakshina" on the last day, and the money so collected is always meant for the same town or city in the form of books freely distributed to the local college boys.

Again, from the Poona Yagna onward, I have been publishing weekly booklets called *Yagna Prasad*, containing a summary of all the discourses. These booklets were distributed free to all those who had given me their names and addresses in all the previous yagnashalas. But slowly, by the time I came to the sixth yagnashala, the total recipients rose up to about 12,000, so that it became beyond the means of any committee to invite the swami for conducting any Yagna. Naturally, I had to drop the *Yagna Prasad*, to give life to the Chinmaya Yagna.

When it came to the discourses on *Geeta*, I had already contacted more than 35,000 devotees, and therefore it was decided that we run a fortnightly magazine to report the *Geeta* talks. Thus, the *Tyagi* magazine came into existence.

Tyagi: The Flow of the *Bhagavad-gītā*

Tyagi, the fortnightly magazine of Chinmaya Mission, was started in September 1955. It continued to carry the symbol of the lighted torch and moved ahead as the 'Organ of the Chinmaya Mission, Madras.' The most important feature of this journal was the serialized talks on the *Bhagavad-gītā*. In fact, this occupied more than half the number of pages in many of the issues where it appeared. It is these articles which were later compiled into the famous book titled *The Holy Geeta*.

Many of Swamiji's talks for the 'All India Radio' found place in the journal in the form of articles. One of the old devotees mentioned some years ago that Swamiji also wrote under the pen name 'Rishikesh,' and indeed the style of those articles in the first few issues seems to vouch for the author's authenticity. Swamiji's commentary on *Ātma Bodha* was also serialized in *Tyagi* in 1958 and then converted into a book.

Articles by Swami Sivananda were featured regularly, besides those by Dr. S. Radhakrishnan, Swami Rama Tirtha, and eminent scholars and spiritual personalities. Swamiji also encouraged devotees to contribute articles as per their understanding.

The English translation of *Himagiri Vihāram* was serialized in *Tyagi*, and later on converted into the book *Wanderings in the Himalayas*. Thus, many of the books published by the Chinmaya Mission are found in their seed-form in *Tyagi*.

Besides articles, *Tyagi* carried a brief 'Mission News' section, which described the major events that had taken place in the various Mission centers, mostly reports of Swamiji's yajñas and talks. It also carried announcements of Swamiji's forthcoming *Jñāna Yajñas*. Slowly, by 1956, Swamiji's itinerary started appearing, too.

TYAGI

144, Mount Road, Madras 6

Editor:
V. R. VIRAMANI, B.A. HONS. (LOND.)

Editorial Committee:
Mrs. Balammal, B.A.
M. G. Subrahmanyan, B.SC.

Art Editor:
D. N. Varadu

Treasurer:
V. Kunjitapadam

Price Single Copy 4 as.
Annual Subscription:
Inland Rs. 6   Foreign 12 sh. or 2.50 $

The income and expenditure accounts of various yajña committees also found place in *Tyagi*, ensuring transparency in accounts. The list of books available for sale was published on the back inner cover.

◄ *The cover page of the* Tyagi *changed and evolved through the years.*

The annual subscription for *Tyagi* was Rs. 6, and Swamiji had instructed that anyone who contributed that much or more as Guru-dakṣiṇā at the *yajñaśālās* should automatically be enrolled as a member and start receiving *Tyagi* regularly. Apparently, *Tyagi* was also posted to places outside India, because the rates advertised were 12 shillings/$2.50 annually.

Tyagi was initially published from Chennai. Then, in February 1957, it was moved to Bengaluru, and in September 1960 to Chittoor, under Śrī Dwaraknath Reddy. From July 1, 1961 (Vol. 6, No. 21), the page dimensions were increased, and it was changed from a fortnightly magazine to a monthly publication.

List of *Tyagi* Editors

1. V. R. Viramani — September 1955 to December 1956
2. G. Natarajan,[4] Honorary Editors K. S. Ramaswamy Sastriar and A. G. Ramachandra Rao — January 1956 to August 1960
3. Dwaraknath Reddy — September 1960 to February 1965

---

[4] G. Natarajan became Swami Dayananda, and later on left Chinmaya Mission to form an organization of his own.

Swamiji was very proactive in propagating the magazine and used every opportunity possible. A letter in his files dated November 29, 1956, shows that the municipal commissioner of Madurai had placed an order for Chinmaya Mission books for use in the public library, and the person in charge of this in the Mission had replied with a copy to Swamiji:

> We also send you herewith our bill for subscription for *Tyagi* for the years beginning 1st September 1955 to 31st August 1956, and 1st September 1956 to 31st August 1957. Please send remittance for this as well.
>
> *Geeta* discourses of Swami Chinmayananda from Chapter 1 find a place in a series in *Tyagi* issues, and it is this that prompted us to take you as a subscriber from its inception. We trust you will appreciate this.

Swamiji maintained regular correspondence with the editors of *Tyagi* and guided them in all matters — content as well as printing, subscriptions, and dispatch. He systematically filed all the communications he received, noting the date of receipt in his own handwriting on the top right-hand side of the first page of the letter. Later, in the early nineties, he handed over all such files to Smt. Leela Nambiar, to be preserved in the office of *Tapovan Prasad*. Now they have been handed over to Chinmaya Archives in the Mumbai Āśrama. One of the files had an original handwritten

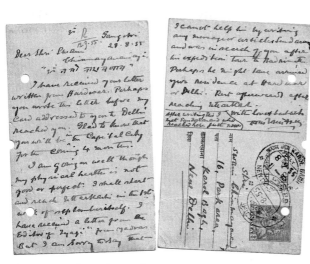

▲ *A postcard written by Swami Tapovan Maharaj to Swami Chinmayananda*

postcard from Swami Tapovan Maharaj to Swami Chinmayananda, referring to a request for articles by the editor of *Tyagi*.

In his inaugural message to the *Tyagi*, Swami Chinmayananda explained the need for the magazine and his vision for it; he also gave precious words of advice to the editorial staff.

I salute the Madras Chinmaya Mission. Your idea of starting a fortnightly spiritual magazine deserves all congratulations. You have given it the name 'Tyagi' and placed it at the disposal of all future yagnashalas where I may give discourses to the ardent devotees. I am extremely grateful for this great seva that you have planned to do for my activities.

It was becoming harder to find a new centre for conducting the yagnas, not because there is not enough enthusiasm, but the enthusiastic members make a quick retreat the moment they hear of the responsibility of publishing about 12,000 *Yagna Prasad* booklets each week for free distribution.

I, too, was feeling that it was unfair to press any centre when I can vividly realize their actual incapacity. In each centre, after a session of a few weeks, many new converts become sincere followers, thirsting to know and panting to practice. Thus, with each yagna, the responsibility of a new centre becomes increased. I was in a sense desperate, not knowing what would be the way out, especially when this yagna scheme has been going on for the last four years without any capital or any reserve to fall back on.

At this juncture, the inspired enthusiasm of the Madras Chinmaya Mission is indeed gloriously divine. The spirit of sacrifice with which many good souls have come around to associate themselves with this endeavour assures me that this is a program divinely blessed by the Rishis of yore, whose eternal voice

▶

we propose to echo above the rumbling voices of this discordant age. Hereafter I have no objection in promising you that all the yagnashala talks will be sent to you for publication in *Tyagi*. ...

I am sure the editorial staff will remember and the contributors will equally keep in mind that *Tyagi* is not a religious tract, but a spiritual magazine trying to provide a forum in which all thinkers of every creed and shade of opinion can ventilate their ideas so that we may discover, as a result of our cooperative effort, a way of better living and the means by which we can make this scheme practical for every man of imagination and courage. Thus will the present spiritual crisis in the world be met, and may *Tyagi* show the torch so that our generation may walk out of the jungle into which they have roamed unwittingly.

I salute the *Tyagi* with Prem and Om.

– Swami Chinmayananda
(Message published in *Tyagi*, Vol. 1, No 1)

One of the highlights of *Tyagi* was the special issue in a bigger size brought out in January 1958, on the occasion of the first anniversary of the Mahāsamādhi of Parama Pūjya Swami Tapovan Maharaj. The precious articles in this collection have been reproduced in *Tapovan Prasad* and other magazines of the Mission.

◀ *The special issue of* Tyagi *brought out to commemorate the first anniversary of the Mahāsamādhi of Swami Tapovan Maharaj*

Here is glorious news for TYAGI readers!

Swami Chinmayanandaji has written a commentary on Bhagavad Geeta specially intended for children. TYAGI will print it in serial form commencing with the issue of January 1964. The first instalment will be the introduction. Thereafter, each month (for 18 months to follow) one chapter of Geeta will be covered.

Originally prepared for Chinmaya Mission Bala-Vihar Children, this work will give all parents a grand opportunity to present the ideas of Geeta to their children in a suitable manner.

Only one who has abiding love for, and deep understanding of, both Bhagavad Geeta and children, could have attempted this commentary— in Swamiji, we have one such.

We invite new readers to become subscribers now. We request our readers to inform their friends. Please write to us before 10th January, so that we may print extra copies to meet the demand.

— *Editor.*

The serialization of *Bhagavad-gītā* in *Tyagi* was completed in the first issue of March 1960, Vol. 5, No. 13, and from the next issue onward, Swamiji's commentary on *Vivekacūḍāmaṇi* was published serially. Swamiji wrote a special commentary on the *Bhagavad-gītā* for children, which was serialized in *Tyagi*, beginning January 1964.

By this time, the new journal, *Tapovan Prasad*, published from Sandeepany Sadhanalaya, Mumbai, had come into its own and was ready to absorb *Tyagi*. However, *Tyagi* continued to be published until February 1965 to complete the serial 'Geeta for the Children,' and then *Tyagi* was merged into the main magazine, *Tapovan Prasad*.

We salute *Tyagi* for the wonderful work that it has done in serving our Mission and in spreading the knowledge. It is through *Tyagi* that I first published my *Geeta* in serial [form]. ...

The Mission work got spread to such dimensions that we felt the necessity for a special organ to describe elaborately and report exhaustively our plans and their execution, and hence we started the *Usha* magazine. When we issued the *Tapovan Prasad* journal from Sandeepany Sadhanalaya, we absorbed *Usha* into it, and yet, *Tyagi* served on as a separate organ, mainly to bring out my 'Geeta for the Children.' It also served as a field where our

▶

Study Group members could express themselves, their spiritual thoughts, and their philosophical reactions.

Sri Dwaraknath Reddy was bringing out the issues regularly against tremendous odds, and the Chinmaya Mission cannot forget the part played by Editor Dwaraknath in maintaining *Tyagi* for the last three years. His editorials have been inspired writing. If they had a touch of poetry, they also had a serious depth of serenity. All the readers have been so well inspired by it that I had volumes of letters of applause for the editor reaching me these few years.

The running subscribers for *Tyagi* will be absorbed into *Tapovan Prasad* ... with effect from February 1965.

– Swami Chinmayananda (Published in *Tyagi*, December 1964, and *Tapovan Prasad*, March 1965)

Usha: Knitting the Fabric of Chinmaya Mission

As the years rolled on, more branches of Chinmaya Mission began to spring up in various towns and cities, and their activities also increased manifold. By 1958, a need was felt for a separate magazine to feature the expanding Mission News, to announce forthcoming programs, and to communicate in general with the devotees who were spread all over India. Swamiji called this magazine *Usha* and said that it signified the 'dawn' of a new era.

With *Usha*, we invoke the dawn of our revival. Renaissance of a culture can be brought about only when the people get inspired by the values of life recommended by it. ...

Therefore, to invoke the 'Usha' of our culture would be to bring the salient features of Hinduism and the inexhaustible beauties of our culture to the understanding of our generation. …

The Mission Groups, except in a few centres, have been multiplying very healthily, and each of them has been taking the torch of knowledge, lit up in the yagnashalas, very faithfully to the different mohallas [areas] of their own cities. Now it is time that the groups come together and their activities get somehow coordinated and systematized — each group drawing its inspiration from its sister groups functioning elsewhere in India. *Usha* will be this messenger; she will contact all groups by her awakening rays!

Usha is meant for encouraging the penmanship of our members. We will certainly give all allowances and give a preference to entertain and publish the articles of our members in *Usha*.

– Swami Chinmayananda
(*Usha*, Vol. 1, No. 1, March 15, 1958)

Regd No. M. 6673

USHA

CHINMAYA MISSION HOUSE MAGAZINE—MONTHLY (ENGLISH)

Annual Subscription ... ... **Rs. 4/- only.**

The USHA will serve as an embrace that will hold us all together reporting the happenings in each group of the Chinmaya Mission.

EDITOR ... *Miss Lakshmi Reddy*

Published by :

Sri. C. Gopal Reddy, Anasuya Villa, Himayat Nagar, Hyderabad and printed at Krishnavas International, Amrit Manzil, Malakpet, Hyderabad.

A. **The monthly will contain :**

1. Reports from each Branch, each Group : Satsangs held, topics discussed. summary of learned discourses listend to. the books read, suggestions of books and summary of their contents etc., for the benefit of the members in other Groups.

2. The anniversary ceremonies and different Sacred-day celebrations conducted. Accounts, Office-bearers appointed etc.

3. Personalities of merit in the Chinmaya family : Short sketches.

4. Photos of functions, spiritual picnics, and other activities.

5. Editorial from Sri Swamiji.

6. Visions and dreams of work—from each member : suggestions and plans.

7. Doubts raised—solutions suggested.

8. Reports of Yagnas—News from Sandeepani Sadhanalaya, the College of Knowledge.

B. All Mission Groups will be subscribers to the monthy. All instructions from Swamiji to the Groups will be published through its pages. Devotees also can be subscribers who are interested in watching over the activities of the Mission.

C. Articles and interesting Spiritual Experiences, Episodes and Happenings from members, *forwarded through the Group leaders*, will be considered for publication.

D. We will accept all advertisements—in the *opening few* inner pages and *last few* pages. Members are requested to help us in canvasing :

Full Page (annual)	Rs. 100	Per insertion	Rs. 10
Half Page (annual)	Rs. 60	Per insertion	Rs. 6

All advertisement materials and payments should be sent to:—

Mrs. Sulochana Reddy, Advertisement-in-Charge, Usha, Anasuya Villa, Himayat Nagar, Hyderabad (Deccan).

All subscriptions may please be addressed to :—

Mrs. Sulakshana Reddy, Treasurer, Usha, 3-4-616, Narayanguda, Hyderabad (Deccan).

The importance of *Usha* was that it knitted the devotees from various corners of India into the fabric of Chinmaya Mission. All the Mission centers were instructed to send reports of their activities to *Usha*. The 'Mission News' section of *Tyagi* moved into *Usha*. Devotees wrote about their pilgrimage to important temples and Āśramas and their encounters with other Mahātmās. There was a section that featured letters to and from children and emphasized higher values, while addressing issues that concerned them. 'Satsangh Hall' was another regular feature with questions and answers or thoughts on a given topic, a kind of extension of the Study Group. 'Sparks from the Yagnashala' gave inspiring samples from Swamiji's latest discourses and informal satsaṅgas. In 1959, some of the articles on spiritual topics pending publication in *Tyagi* were sent to *Usha*, as pressure was building up to complete the commentary on the *Bhagavad-gītā* in *Tyagi*.

◀ *Swamiji sent this instruction to Smt. Lakshmi Reddy to prepare the compilation of his* Usha *editorials into the book* As I Think.

In spite of the hectic schedule of yajñas, satsaṅgas and travel, Swamiji made time to write the editorials himself. A collection of these editorials was brought out in book form, titled *As I Think*, as early as November 1959. However, he stopped writing the editorials from the August 1960 issue of *Usha*, and instead started publishing his commentary on *Badarīśa Stotram* by Swami Tapovan Maharaj. This grew into the full-fledged book, *Hymn to Badrinath*, as we know it today.

▲ *Smt. Lakshmi Reddy is seated at Gurudev's feet, along with other devotees.*

Usha was published from Hyderabad, and the editor's mantle fell on Smt. Lakshmi Reddy, who used to sing bhajans and often chant the ślokas at Swamiji's yajñas. She continued as editor until the end, when the magazine merged into *Tapovan Prasad* in October 1963. Meticulously and carefully, she preserved every photo sent with captions handwritten at the back by Swamiji. Those have now been handed over to Chinmaya Archives, along with letters numbering more than one hundred, written by Swamiji to her.

Swamiji's Role in Other Magazines

Before we proceed further, it must be mentioned that much before *Tyagi* and *Usha*, Swamiji had been the co-editor of a magazine named *Call Divine*, published by Śrī Ramana Satchidananda Mandali, a group of devotees of Śrī Ramana Bhagavan, based in Mumbai. The first issue in September 1952 names Swamiji as the joint editor with Swami Rajeshwarananda, who later contributed some articles to *Tyagi* as well. It was for the

▲ *Swami Chinmayananda and Swami Rajeshwara-nanda*

Ramana Jayanti January 1953 issue of this magazine that Swamiji had requested an article from Swami Tapovan Maharaj, about his meeting with Bhagavan Ramana Maharshi many years ago. This is the famous article that begins: "Silence is Truth ...."

Silence is Truth. Silence is Bliss. Silence is Peace. And hence Silence is Atman. Such a silence or to be established in such a silence is the ultimate goal of all spiritualism. It is Moksha. It is the end of this endless cycle of births and deaths. Sri Ramana Maharshi was an embodiment of such a silence or he was Silence itself. Therefore he did not preach Silence. He was not a preacher of Silence. He could not preach Silence. When one becomes away from Silence, he can preach Silence. How can Silence itself preach Silence.

Nearly 35 or 40 years ago, I had the good fortune of having the Darshan of Maharshi at Tiruvannamalai when he was living there in a cave along with his mother and brother. One mid-day, I, a young Brahmacharin at that time, climbed to the cave, saw the Maharshi there,

▲ *The first page of a handwritten message sent by Swami Tapovan Maharaj to Swami Chinmayananda for the Ramana Jayanti issue of* Call Divine *magazine, January 1953*

Advertisement of Call Divine *magazine edited by Swami Chinmayananda*

THE "CALL DIVINE"

A MONTHLY DEDICATED TO

BHAGVAN SRI RAMANA

EDITED BY
SWAMI CHINMAYANANDA

Annual Subscription Rs. 3/–

PUBLISHED AT
1/8, BHUTA NIVAS,
MATUNGA, BOMBAY–19.

Though Swamiji continued to be named the editor until the end of the decade, his active contribution was confined to the early years of the magazine's inception. He wrote a series of articles, which were published under the title 'Talks with Aspirants.'

Swami Chinmayananda's letterhead as editor of the Call Divine ▼

Swami Chinmayananda (UTTERKASI).
EDITOR "THE CALL DIVINE"

P. Bhaskara menon.
Ernakulam.

Yagnasala.
W. E. A.
Karol Bagh.
New Delhi 5.
14-12-53.

LISTEN TO THE "CALL" FROM GURUVAYOOR

A sister publication of the Mission organs is being published from Guruvayoor. A Hindu-cultural-religious magazine, broad-based on Indian Philosophy, the monthly journal is to be simultaneously published in English and Malayalam under the captions "The Divine call" and "Sankh-Nadam" respectively. The members of the Mission and other enthusiasts of Hindu learning are requested to accord the journal a warm welcome by contributing articles and subscribing to it. H. H. Swami Chinmayananda is the Chief Editor for both these journals.

Address your mails to :
Sri S. P. Nair,
Sri Guruvayoorappan Publications (P) Ltd.,
GURUVAYOOR (Kerala.)

Two magazines, titled *The Divine Call* and *Sankha Nadam*, in English and Malayalam respectively, were published from Guruvayoor with Swami Chinmayananda as the chief editor. Not much is known about them, nor how long they functioned.

◄ Advertisement of The Divine Call *and* Sankha Nadam *that appeared in* Tyagi, *July 1, 1960*

Letters: Words That Winged Their Way into Devoted Hearts

It is well known that Swami Chinmayananda wrote thousands of letters to his devotees during his lifetime. Through these words, he planted in their hearts seeds that sprouted — sometimes after many years. He was methodical and indefatigable in replying promptly to letters.

Day after day he wrote, coaxing and cajoling, admonishing and guiding, consoling and comforting, encouraging and inspiring, teaching and clarifying doubts — the letters flowed out into the world in many directions to accomplish their work. At the time of this writing, they are being collected by Chinmaya Archives, and we watch in wonder at the growing pile, which has already crossed 15,000! We will never know how many he wrote, because many have not been preserved, many have just dissolved and merged into the minds of devotees, and many have flown with the tide of time.

As early as 1958, there was a request through *Tyagi* to the readers, asking them for letters that could be included in the section "Talks with Aspirants." The first collection of letters was published as a book in 1959, titled *Vedanta through Letters*. After many years, a second volume was published in 1996. At the launch of the Chinmaya Centenary Celebrations in May 2015, a coffee table book *Yours Forever: Life and Letters of Swami Chinmayananda* was released.

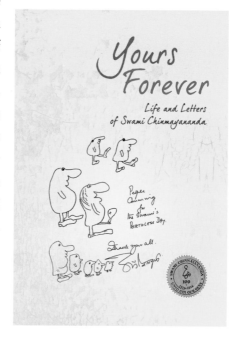

Two sisters Bina and Meena Chakraburtty received their instructions very clearly in a letter dated September 3, 1976:

It is **not** right that you two **don't** go to school just because Swamiji has come. Religion and spiritual living should make the devotee more conscientious and dutiful towards life. Your duties now are to study and attend classes. That is your dharma. You should **never give up** your dharma.

Pujya Gurudev encouraged people to start Balavihars and gave them clear guidelines about how to handle the children.

Children recognises and appreciates much more readily the love and sincerity is there. Pour out your love and sincerity to them: yet be strict for their own descipline. They will be a little wild in the beginning. Soon they will be quite and nice. The juniors allow them more freedom than for teenagers.

Promila Modi 26.9.1972

Children recognise and appreciate much more readily the love and sincerity in others. Pour out your love and sincerity to them: yet be strict for their own discipline. They will be a little wild in the beginning: soon they will be quiet and nice. The juniors: allow them more freedom than for teenagers.

71

▲ *A page from the book* Yours Forever

PART TWO

THE TRUNK

The Trunk

Commentaries on the Upaniṣads

Swamiji came down from Uttarkashi and began the saga of jñāna yajñas with great spiritual fervor. He started with the Upaniṣads, which enshrined the subtlest teachings of Vedāntic scriptures. At the first yajña in Pune, he expounded on the *Kenopaniṣad* and the *Kaṭhopaniṣad*. At the next four yajñas held in Madras (now Chennai), Delhi, Palakkad, and Madurai, he gave discourses on *Muṇḍakopaniṣad*, *Māṇḍūkyopaniṣad*, *Īśāvāsyopaniṣad*, and *Praśnopaniṣad*, respectively. In 1955, he talked on *Taittirīya Upaniṣad* and *Aitareya Upaniṣad* in Madras and Kozhikode respectively.

All these talks were recorded in the *Yagna Prasad* booklets. These booklets became very popular and there was a great demand for them; hence, they were compiled into regular books. Sometimes, at the end of the yajña in any given place, Swamiji used to stay on for a few extra days to complete the *Yagna Prasad* booklet, and give his final revising touches so that they could be easily converted into a book. Thus, by 1955, Swamiji's commentaries on most of the major Upaniṣads were available as books and could be used as texts at subsequent yajñas.

The books followed a standardized format, starting with the introduction, which was sometimes quite exhaustive. Then the original mantras of the Upaniṣads were printed in Sanskrit, one at a time, followed by the transliteration into English, the individual word meanings, the translation, and then the detailed commentary.

Printing books and distributing them free of cost was not easy. During the first yajña in Pune, the printing of the *Yagna Prasad* booklets began with great enthusiasm, but soon the financial crunch was felt. In the last booklet, which contained the final instalment of the commentary on the *Kenopaniṣad*, Swamiji announced, "For the time being, the Poona Committee will not be in a position to undertake any more expenditure on publishing the *Prasads* which are to report the discourses on the *Kathopanishad* mantras. If and when, during these yagna days, we are blessed by the voluntary cooperation of any Lakshminarayan, we shall at once resume our publications."

Many devotees were fired with enthusiasm and came forward with their contributions to meet the financial requirements. But, in and through it all, Swamiji's cousin Śrī Bhaskara Menon extended his help wholeheartedly during those early years, not only pitching in with financial support whenever needed, but also helping with the printing, storing, and distribution of books.

Chief Priest
H. H. SREE SWAMI CHINMAYANANDA

276 Rasta Peth,
Poona 2.

Children Of Light,
THWAME-VAHA-MASMI!!

Salutations and prostrations to the Immortal Saints and Sages of the Upanishads! May they ever bless us with more and more ampler chances of serving them!! The Divine satisfaction that this Sevak feels at having fulfilled his mission so far, to the best of his ability, is a reward too high for the actual turnover of the work. His thanks are indeed due to him who lives in His manifestation as you all.

With this Number of the YAGNA PRASAD we are completing our study of KENOPANISHAD. At the Yagna Sala we are progressing industriously forward and have reached almost the end of the first *Valli* in KATHOPNISHAD.

For the time being the Poona Committee will not be in a position to undertake anymore expenditure on publishing the *Prasads* which are to report the discourses on *Kathopanishad Mantras*. If and when, during these Yagna days, we are blessed by the voluntary cooperation of any LAKSHMINARAYAN, we shall at once resume our publications.

So, till then good-bye. The committee shall be contacting you the moment they can again discover enough *Ishwar Kripa* to serve you all.

With hopes of getting more and more chances to serve you all, and with prem and pranam.

Thy Own Self,
CHINMAYANANDA.

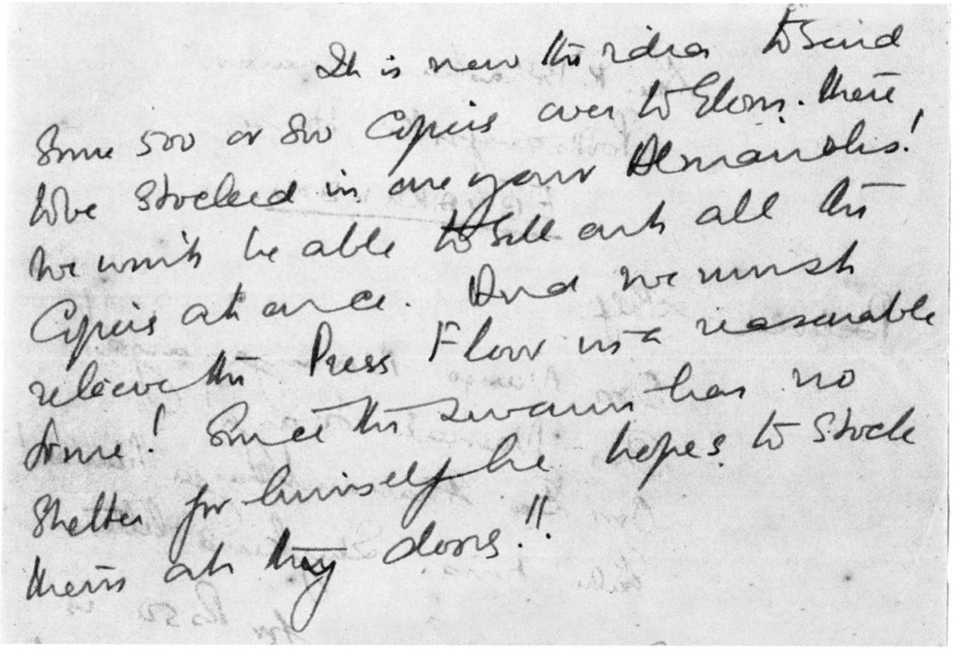

[handwritten letter facsimile]

On August 21, 1952, Swamiji writes to him, "It is now the idea to send some 500 or 800 copies over to Ernakulam, there to be stocked in one of your almairahs [cupboards]! We won't be able to sell out all the copies at once. And we must relieve the press floor in a reasonable time! Since the Swami has no shelter for himself, he hopes to stock them at thy doors!" In another letter in May 1955, he instructs, "Packets of books will be coming by train from Kozhikode in your name, which you have to stock in a place safely away from hungry rats and white ants. Those books are to go to Trivandrum with us."

Swamiji wrote to his cousin almost every day and shared, through hundreds of letters, his daily concerns.

▲ *Bhaskara Menon*

In a letter dated June 20, 1952, he wrote, "Thousand five hundred rupees to be given to the press-men one month after delivery of the books!! And the Swami has not now 15 pies (paise) to call his own!! But the Lord is great; scores of times He had been showing that His ways are strange and ever new!! With all faith and devotion, Chinmaya is waiting to see in what ways Lord's next leela plays itself out!!"

Swamiji gave instructions to Bhaskara Menon about the minutest aspects of the work on hand. How hard he worked can be seen clearly from a letter written to his cousin on September 3, 1952:

> This is the 34th letter written this day — yes, day because it is already 2 A.M.!! — after nine hours proofreading in a soul-killing noisy printing house during the day hours!! If Chinmaya is not dying now, it is because he is already dead!! Tired. Tired. Tired. Yet in all joy — for is not this body dedicated to His seva!!

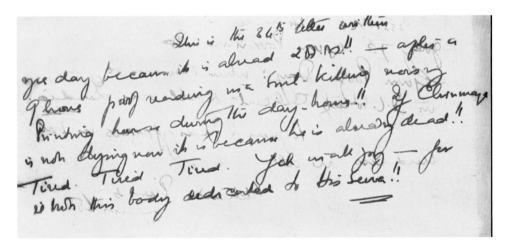

Shiela Puri of Delhi was another major supporter in the early years of publication. Sheela Sharma of Rewa, who translated the books into Hindi, worked in close coordination with Shiela Puri, with clear instructions from Swamiji. These early pioneers were the pillars of the publication work that Swamiji considered so important in spreading the message of Vedānta.

[handwritten note]

◀ *From a letter to Sheela Sharma dated April 21, 1955*

❝ *Will you please parcel the Meditation and Life of yours immediately to Mrs. Puri, 4 Jantar Mantar Road, New Delhi. Your translation must be much better than the one we have got there.*

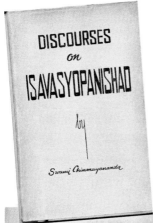

For a Third Time

I am extremely happy to bring out Isa of Sri Chinmaya for the third time. No doubt we have crossed miles and miles of the lower planes of our own moral and spiritual decadence during these past six years which I call "The Chinmaya Era"—the era that started with his first Upanishad Yagna in 1952 at Poona. The persistent demand for his books, the countless youthful rounded hands that ceaselessly stretch forth at the Yagna-Shala Counters when the books are exchanged, all these assure us that Sri Chinmaya's Voice is being heard by the growing younger generation.

I bring out this third edition with all prayers unto Him who gave us our guide and Master in Sri Swamiji.

42, Asoka Road,
NEW DELHI,
31st March 1959.   MRS. SHIELA PURI.

Preface to Second Edition

IN publishing this Second Edition of the ISAVASYOPANI-SHAD, I have great pleasure to announce that it has been slightly enlarged and perceptibly improved upon by Shri Swami Chinmayanandaji himself. Suggestions from Readers have been incorporated wherever found necessary and we are bringing out this Second Edition in the hope that we will be serving the greater demands for the Spiritual Text-Books that are now hardly available in this country.

Shri Swami Chinmayanandaji's Books, as you all know, have never been placed in the Book-Stalls of open market place. We are publishing these books only for limited circulation to serve mainly Swamiji's direct disciples. The First Edition went off the shelf mainly in free distribution although a few copies have been sold. These free distributions were mainly done in the Delhi University, during the 1955 Convocation Day. Many copies were, of course, given out by Swamiji to deserving seekers in his fold.

In this re-modelled edition, our great aim is to bring the lucid explanations of these *mantras* to the notice of the educated in our generation. We are sure that as in the past we will be ever receiving encouragement and patronage from all quarters in this our noble endeavour.

Dissemination of the Knowledge of our Scriptures is the greatest charity that a man can ever do in his life. There is nothing nobler than *Vidyadan*.

4, Jantar Mantar Road,
NEW DELHI,
January 1, 1956.   MRS. SHIELA PURI,
Publisher.

The Holy Geeta

By the latter half of 1955, Swamiji started conducting full-fledged jñāna yajñas on various chapters of the *Bhagavad-gītā*. While he periodically gave discourses on the Upaniṣads as the main texts in some places, he slowly shifted the focus to the *Bhagavad-gītā*, because he found that the general public responded better to the way the message was presented in the *Gītā*. Gradually, the Upaniṣads were reserved for the morning classes, where admission was restricted to Mission members and advanced students of Vedānta.

At the beginning, the talks on the *Gītā* were published as a series in *Tyagi*. But soon it was time for the series to be converted into book form. By March 1959, notices started appearing in *Usha*: "Discourses on the *Bhagavad Geeta* (Vol. 1) are getting ready." By June 1959, the first volume, consisting of the commentary on the first five chapters, was ready; sales were brisk. The second volume began to be dispatched by September 1959.

The November 1959 issue of *Usha* carried the announcement: "Good Glorious News — Swamiji

DISCOURSES ON

THE BHAGAWAD GEETA

BY
SWAMI CHINMAYANANDA

First Volume is getting ready

This contains the first five chapters—Stanzas in *Devanagari* script with Roman transliteration—Word to word meaning for each stanza followed by paraphrase and commentary. The exhaustive discourse by Swamiji on each stanza covers a wide field of human knowledge like philosophy, religion, culture, society and human psychology. It is a commentary on Life! Beautifully got up in an easy-to-handle size of ¼ crown.

GEETA IN THREE VOLUMES

Ordinary edition : Vol. I—Rs. 7/-, Vol. II—Rs. 4/-, Vol. III—Rs. 4/-.

De-lux edition : In Real Art—Rs. 50/- per set. (The sale-proceeds of this edition will go to make the ordinary edition cheap).

Reserve your set by remitting Rs. 15/- or Rs. 50/- to :
Sri T. P. Sundaram,
Chinmaya Nilayam, 16, Harrington Road, Madras-31.

(Postage free for those who advance for the whole set). The cost of the ordinary edition per set is Rs. 15/- only, not Rs. 20/- as announced recently in the USHA. Such of those as have already sent Rs. 20/- and reserved their sets, will get Rs. 5/- refunded.

◄ *Announcement in Tyagi, May 1, 1959*

◄ *Published in* Tyagi, *October 15, 1959*

has concluded dictating his *Geeta* discourses at Madurai on Deepavali Day, October 31, 1959. Total manuscript runs into 2085 foolscap pages double line typing. He started dictating his notes on the *Geeta* in 1955 and started simultaneously the journal *Tyagi*. From September 1955 onwards *Tyagi* has been publishing these *Geeta* notes regularly." And this stupendous work was done between a tight schedule of yajñas, travel, and work on his pet dream of Sandeepany Sadhanalaya, institute of Vedānta at Powai, Mumbai.

The first edition of *The Holy Geeta* in three volumes was printed in Chennai at Hoe and Company. Śrī V. Sethuram took charge of collecting the material and seeing it through the process of printing. The response was so good that by 1961, an enlarged edition in four volumes was brought out. Readers expressed their appreciation and lavished praise.

In response to one such effusive feedback, Swamiji wrote:

> When a great speaker, painter or musician receives the wildest applause at the end of an inspired evening's performance; whoever he be, he sincerely denies the fact that he did consciously deliver the speech, or consciously sung the song, or deliberately planned and worked out the painting. Moments of inspiration are moments of self-forgetfulness, and they come only when the individual is completely tuned up with the theme of his heart. And thereafter, the art takes charge of him and express itself through the given medium of expressions chosen by the particular artist. In spiritual life too when the teacher is galloping high into the highest peaks of inspired living, in those sacred moments of thrilled meditations, he individually ceases to function, and he explodes to express his mighty realisation in the joyous language of the Gods, These declarations become the scriptures of the world, and these have an endless potency to widen their embrace to accommodate the entire mankind.
>
> —*Swami Chinmaya.*

Edition after edition of the book was rolled out. Through the years, *The Holy Geeta* gained the status of a scripture in itself because the commentary brought the message of the *Bhagavad-gītā* to all educated people. No more was the holy text relegated to the pūjā room, only to be worshiped with flowers and never to be opened and read! Attending Swamiji's lectures on the *Gītā* became the hallmark of all intellectuals. People gathered in thousands to listen to him, and in the hands of each person in the audience was a copy of *The Holy Geeta*. For their convenience, individual chapters were published as separate slim volumes, easy to carry wherever they went.

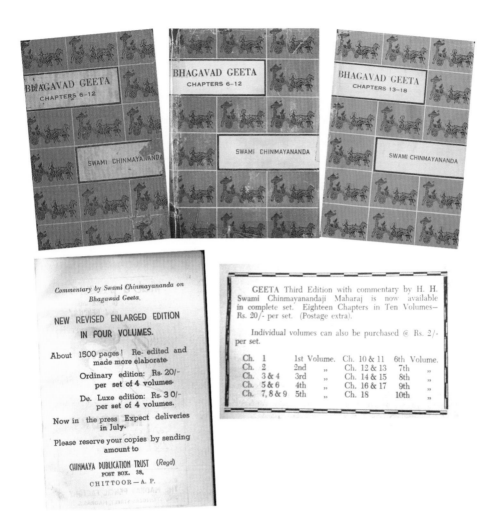

Since then, *The Holy Geeta* has been translated into many regional languages, the most important of them being the translation into Hindi, done personally by Swami Tejomayananda.

In the early seventies, Swamiji decided to place *The Holy Geeta* in the rooms of all major hotels. "In all the hotels I go to, they have the Bible. In India, we should have the *Gītā*," said Swamiji. Thus, even people who may not have ever read it would also leaf through it, at least casually. And those who cherished the sacred book would have a pleasant surprise seeing it on the table in their hotel rooms.

He entrusted Bharati Sukhatankar with the task of turning the four-volume book into a single volume, edited to suit an international readership. He wanted the verses to be printed only in English, not in Sanskrit. Further, the verses were moved to the bottom of the page to facilitate the smooth flow of the commentary. He told her to remove repetitions and colloquial words and phrases.

Even before the contents page, Swamiji provided a practical list titled 'The Essence of Geeta: Direct Guidance for Your Problems,' which indicated the verses where one could look for solutions to specific problems like 'Consolation for the (1) Bereaved (2) Disillusioned ...' and 'Guidance to (1) Politicians (2) Businessmen (3) Teenagers,' and so on. This continues to be printed in the latest editions of the book. This feature has helped many a reader to connect with the sacred text in a useful and practical manner.

Swamiji gave instructions for this special edition to be printed on onion-skin paper so that the entire book would be compact and elegant. Śrī Ram Batra, who published the book, observed: "Swamiji, all this is good, but people might take it away from the hotel room!" Swamiji turned and looked into his eyes and said, "*That* is the whole idea." Hotels were instructed to regularly inform CCMT[1] how many copies of the book had been taken away, and they would be replaced promptly. The expenses were borne by CCMT, not the hotels.

By the end of 1973, Swamiji had handed over 750 copies of this special edition to Taj Intercontinental, Bombay. No one will ever know how many thousands of people were touched by the sacred text in this way. In many hotels, it became the norm to place a copy of the *Gītā* in their rooms. Today, many hotels purchase *The Holy Geeta* in bulk every year.

▲ *Śrī Ram Batra, secretary of CCMT, hands over a copy of* The Holy Geeta *to Śrī A. B. Kelkar, managing director of Taj Intercontinental. Looking on is Śrī Jamnadas Moorjani, trustee of CCMT.*

---

[1]   Central Chinmaya Mission Trust

HOLY GEETA PRESENTATION TO TAJ MAHAL HOTEL, BOMBAY.

Seven hundred fifty copies of the Holy Geeta have been presented to the Taj-Inter-continental, Bombay, for placement in individual rooms for the benefit of tourists, foreign, as well as Indian, by the Central Chinmaya Mission Trust (CCMT). The 1,200-pages volume, printed in special featherweight paper, is a cloth-bound, gold embossed, gilt-edged book which has elicited encomiums from numerous recipients. The Central Chinmaya Trust plans to place this volume individual rooms of all major hotels in India. A few copies have also been set apart for the general public at a reasonable price of Rs. 30/- per copy, plus postage (Rs. 3/-).

Śrī K. C. Patnaik recalls:

> Soon after joining CCMT, when I went to Delhi, I visited some bookshops to see whether they had stocked any of our publications. The moment they came to know that I had come from CCMT, they almost mobbed me, asking for *The Holy Geeta*. They were selling the book for double the price because there was such a demand and copies were not easily available. After I returned, we purchased some 7–8 lakhs rupees worth of the special thin paper and reprinted the book to meet the heavy demand.

The Holy Geeta has been translated into many languages and is also available in Braille. It has also been presented in small excerpts in the online courses of Chinmaya International Foundation. The story of its journey in visual medium is traced in the section on the Chinmaya Video Dham in the next chapter.

Vivekacūḍāmaṇi

In the mid-fifties, as the process of jñāna yajñas continued, Swamiji realized the need to teach the basics of Vedānta and began to give talks on *Ātma Bodha* and the first 100 verses of *Vivekacūḍāmaṇi*, both of which were serially printed in *Tyagi* and later published in book form. The rest of *Vivekacūḍāmaṇi*, which has a total of 581 verses, had to wait until 1970 to be completed and published as a book. That is a story in itself.

In the preface to the book, written on Guru Pūrṇimā Day, July 18, 1970, Swamiji explains the origin:

It has been a painful ecstasy all through the preparation of this manuscript — painful because the commentaries were written during a confusingly long period of the last three or four years. I had first brought out the opening hundred verses in a volume, but, thereafter, the pressure of work being so great, I could not find the necessary leisure for cogently expressing the pregnant suggestions of these brilliant verses of Ācārya Śaṅkara.

In order to drive home the philosophic meaning of these subtle verses, while talking to my students in Sandeepany Sadhanalaya, I often had to repeat myself and, at times, I had even indulged myself in lengthy digressions. These lectures were taped.

All these furlongs of tapes were carefully and laboriously taken by Miss Kanta (Hawaii) with her tape recorder, and they were all industriously transcribed by two diligent members of the Mission — Sri Bhatia (Godrej) and Sri Radhakrishnan (Railways). These voluminous manuscripts were sent to Uttarkashi when I was last there, and to chop and slice them into shape was, in fact, more laborious than dictating the entire lot afresh.

In the final editing and preparation of the manuscript, Miss Bharathi Naik (now Bharati Sukhatankar) helped me with great devotion.

> I am conscious that there are very many jerks along the march of the commentaries upon these verses. Very often the style has conspicuously changed, and the treatment of the verses differs at more than one place in the text. I am conscious of these weaknesses, but I cannot help them as I had to take up the work between long intervals of suffocating work of the yajñaśālās.

What Swamiji does not mention in the preface is that he had a major heart attack in Mysore in March 1970 and spent many weeks in the hospital. In May, he went to the Chinmaya Mission Hospital in Bangalore to recuperate, and by the first week of June, he was back in Bombay convalescing and, at the same time, editing and shaping his commentary on *Vivekacūḍāmaṇi*. By the end of July, the book was ready for publication. Let us hear the rest of the story directly from Smt. Bharati Sukhatankar:

> When Swamiji was convalescing after his heart attack in Bombay, I went and stayed with him for three months. The full first floor of a building, called Usha Kiran on Carmichael Road, was rented for Swamiji. It was a fifteen-story building, and was the highest building in Bombay then. On the opposite side of the road (Pedder Road), the Rohira sisters — Indira and Pushpa — and others used to live. The sisters used to come and cook for him every day. Swamiji liked their cooking a lot, especially the chapatis.
>
> In the flat, three of us stayed with Swamiji — Rama Reddy from Bangalore, who used to take care of his medicines, Sivaraman, who attended to his personal needs, and I, to do the editing work. Early in the morning, Pushpa and the others used to come by.
>
> We used to go for a drive in a limousine at five o'clock in the morning. Śrī Jamnadas drove and Swamiji made me sit in front with him. Swamiji would tell me to read the *Vivekacūḍāmaṇi* manuscript. He would stop me every now and then to say, "Don't put it like this," or "Change that."

We used to drive out of Bombay and then stop somewhere to have breakfast. Kamala Aunty (Kamala Chanrai) brought breakfast. Swamiji liked her cheese toasts — tasty toasties — and coffee. And on the way back, sometimes he would get into the mood to visit people — Anandamayi Maa, Guruji Golwalkar, who was suffering from breast cancer, Ācārya Rajaneesh, who was not called Osho or Bhagavan then. When we visited Anandamayi Maa, she had just entered her room after bathing and her hair was still wet and she had a nice orange towel. Swamiji had a good chat with her, and as we were leaving, she took the towel and put it around Swamiji. I kept eyeing it in the car, hoping that he would give it to me. Swamiji must have read my thoughts, and he promptly gave it to Kamala Aunty!

In the evenings, sometimes Kamala Aunty would drop by. There were others, too — one was a Sindhi girl, also called Kamala. Jamnadas and all of us would sit around, but the doctors had strictly forbidden Swamiji to speak. In those days there was no television, no other means of passing time.

One day, Swamiji had an idea — one of us had to tell a story every evening. We used to be in such a tizzy as each evening approached. Whose turn was it? What story to tell? Where to get a story or how to manufacture one? How to tell it in front of the master storyteller! Swamiji was so good at painting word pictures.

Now we have a lot of resource material. There are many books; we can hunt for stories on the internet. In those days, there was nothing. But Swamiji was very kind. He would say, "I will polish you in the art of storytelling." As we were telling the story, he would stop us in the middle, "Wait a minute; wait a minute! Just fatten this up a little." Sometimes he would say, "You are going too fast." Sometimes he would wait for us to finish and then remark, "When you were describing nature, you should have taken a little more time to make it come alive, to make the listeners visualize what you were saying." Or else he would point out that we were losing the tempo by elaborating too much at a certain juncture. We had to keep the listener's

▲ *Very gently and lovingly, Pūjya Gurudev trained Bharati in editing skills.*

attention riveted. He also told us to establish eye contact. We learned so much from him.

In the afternoons, after we returned from the drive, he had to rest. He would lie down, make me sit at the foot of the bed and read the commentary on the *Vivekacūḍāmaṇi*. These were the recorded talks delivered in Uttarkashi to the first batch of brahmacārīs in 1968. Swami Purushottamananda, Swamini Saradapriyananda, and Swami Jyotirmayananda were among the students then. And the stack of transcribed manuscripts came to me. He told me, "This has to be made into a book. Take out all the colloquialisms and digressions so that it reads like a book and not a lecture." I did it, and then had to read out the edited version to him.

The whole process took quite some time. He taught me the art of editing as well. When I started my course in journalism some years ago, he had written to me, giving all the symbols used in editing, along with elaborate instructions.

A Bouquet of Books

By 1960, a decade after Swamiji began his work, an impressive array of books had already been published. Among these was *Meditation and Life*, a compilation of Swamiji's instructions on meditation while guiding the seekers regularly in the yajñaśālā. This book proved to be invaluable for seekers at all stages of spiritual evolution and hence became very popular. It is in great demand even today.

Hasten Slowly was brought out in installments as newsletters in 1968 and mailed to all the Mission centers. "Swamiji would send the material from Uttarkashi and we would print them in Delhi," says Bharati Sukhatankar. "Later they brought the installments out in book form. *Hasten Slowly* was originally named by Swamiji as 'Bhageerathi Banks Bulletin' or 'BBB' for short. When I wrote that acronym for the first time, Swamiji remarked that it sounded like something from a bank! In the course of time, *Hasten Slowly* was incorporated into *Meditation and Life* — as the final section."

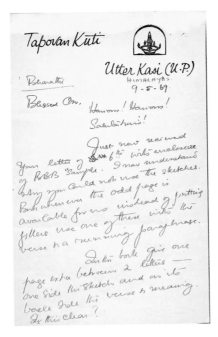

Just now received your letter of 6th with enclosure of BBB sample I now understand why you could not use the sketches. But whenever the odd page is available for us, instead of putting fillers, use one of these with the verse and a running paraphrase.

In the book, give one page extra between two letters — one side the sketch and on its back side the verse and meaning. Is this clear?

ॐ *Just now got BBB No 1. It
is beautifully brought out
and your proof-reading is good.
You are a journalist.*

*The "Banks" looks like and
reads as though a bulletin from
some Bank Ltd.!! Never mind.
In the book we shall give it
the name Meditation: Hasten
Slowly.*

Though *I Love You* was in the form of letters addressed to the Bala Vihar children, it provided material for thought to the sevikās and other adult readers. Swamiji was in retreat at Uttarkashi then (1968), and he called this series of letters a 'Dūta Yajña,' meaning 'Yajña by Post.'

During the periods spent in Uttarkashi, Swamiji wrote commentaries on Swami Tapovan Maharaj's compositions *Ganga Stotram* and *Hymn to Badrinath*. These were also edited by Bharati Sukhatankar and Urmila (Ursula Zieschang).

By 1960, when the second volume of *Hail Renaissance* was published, many of the books had already run through two or three editions, and some, like the English commentaries on *Kenopaniṣad* and *Kaṭhopaniṣad*, had been reprinted four times. The smaller booklets were printed in thousands for distribution at the yajñaśālā. *Meditation and Life* was so popular that it was translated into five languages.

Swamiji had also captured the interest of the intelligentsia in the universities as early as 1953, when he was invited to Poona University for talks. He arranged for free distribution of *Meditation and Life* in

Delhi University in 1955. He kindled the interest of the students by using interactive methods and discussions. He initiated an essay competition in Delhi University on 'My Religion' and invited entries to be sent to the editor of *Tyagi*.

Rules of the Competition :

1. The Essay shall not exceed 50 foolscap pages.
2. It must be typed, double space, one side only.
3. Competitors are not bound by anything that Swamiji said in his discourses; may even refute his views if they can.
4. Essays must reach the Editor, 'TYAGI', 144 Mount Road, Madras-6, not later than March 31st 1956.
5. Essays will be returned, if so desired, but only if accompanied by sufficient stamps and a self-addressed envelope.
6. First prize Rs. 100; Second prize Rs. 50.

By 1960, thirty-nine books had been published and they were handed over to the Chinmaya Publication Trust in 1961.

1. *Vedānta through Letters*
2. *Kaṭhopaniṣad* – English, Telugu, Hindi
3. *Īśāvāsya Upaniṣad* – English, Hindi, Tamil
4. *Kenopaniṣad* – English, Hindi, Tamil, Malayalam
5. *Taittirīya Upaniṣad* – English
6. *Muṇḍakopaniṣad* – English, Telugu, Hindi
7. *Aitareya Upaniṣad* – English, Kannada
8. *Vivekacūḍāmaṇi* – English, Malayalam
9. *Meditation and Life* – English, Telugu, Hindi, Gujarati, Tamil
10. *Hail Renaissance*, Volume 1

11. *Your Life Is Yours*

12. *Māṇḍūkyopaniṣad* and *Kārikā* – English, Hindi

13. *Praśnopaniṣad* – English, Hindi

14. *Ātma Bodha* – English, Tamil, Malayalam

15. *Hinduism at a Glance*

16. *Japa Yoga and Gāyatrī* – English, Tamil

17. *Talks with Aspirants*

18. *Meet Our Gītā*

19. *Flashes on Vedānta*

20. *Vedānta: Bird's Eye-View*

21. *Vedānta through the Glasses of Reason and Logic*

22. *Source of Joy*

23. *The Way*

24. *The Gateway*

25. *The Goal*

26. *Hindu Mata Rahasyam*

27. *As I Think*

28. *Wisdom Capsules*

29. *(Hinduism) at a Glance*

30. *A Peep into Vedānta*

31. *Do We Need Religion?*

32. *Discourses on Gītā (The Holy Geeta)* in three volumes

33. *Hail Renaissance,* Volume 2

34. *Himagiri Vihāra*

35. *Īśvara Darśanam*

36. *Art of Action*

37. *Enquiry of the Human Body*

38. *Aid to Sādhanā*

39. *Prayers unto Him*

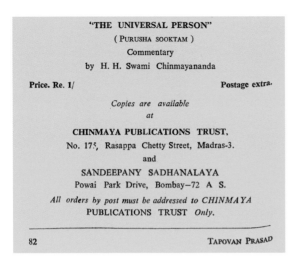

Gurudev's commentary on *Kaivalyopaniṣad* appeared as a series from July 1961 onward in *Tyagi* and was published as a printed volume soon after. Book after book flowed out in a rich cascade to nourish the hungry seekers and devotees. Commentaries on *Viṣṇu Sahasranāma, Nārada Bhakti Sūtram*, and *Puruṣa Sūktam* were published in 1969, and the sale price was ₹6, ₹3.50, and ₹1.

Devotees looked forward with a lot of excitement to the release of each book. The first copy to be released was covered in rich brocaded silk or colorful satin cloth that expressed the tremendous love and enthusiasm of the dedicated workers. The 'Golden Jubilee Yajña' special edition of *Kaṭhopaniṣad* was brought out in a grand and befitting manner during the 51st Jñāna Yajña in Hyderabad, with a golden cover embossed with the logo of the Chinmaya Mission lamp symbol.

Aṣṭāvakra Gītā was released in 1972 by the Governor of Madras, Śrī K. K. Shah, in a special function at Abbotsbury on Mount Road.

Chinmaya Publication Trust

In March 1961, the Chinmaya Publication Trust was registered in Madras (now Chennai). The trust deed[2] states that fifty-nine books by Swami Chinmayananda were handed over to the Trust. The Trust was located in the office of Śrī Govind Das B. Parekh, 175 Rasappa Chetty Street, Park Town, Madras, an address that became quite famous as the focal point of all Chinmaya publications in those days. Śrī Govind Das, who was already doing much of the publication work, was made the administrative trustee and handled all orders for books, dispatch, accounting, maintenance of stock, and reprints. Śrī Anantaraman, his accountant, participated enthusiastically in the work. Śrī V. Sethuram was the Publications Trustee and got many of the books, including the initial publication of *The Holy Geeta* in three volumes, printed by Hoe and Company, where he worked.

For *SADHANA*
For *STUDY*
the Synthesis of SPIRITUAL EVOLUTION
The Illumining
and Long-Awaited Discourses by SREE SWAMIJI
on the Highest Art of Making-Love
to the Lord of the Heart
ORDER your COPIES Today   Single Copy : Rs. 3.5
Books Department :   Sandeepany Sadhanalaya
Powai Park Drive — Bombay 72
MISSION CENTRES — especially where this Text has been taken — ar
advised to order in bulk consignment for their members' study an
savings in postage.

▲ *Announcement in* Tapovan Prasad, *March 1968*

By the early sixties, the Powai āśrama had come up and was becoming the center of activities. The *Tapovan Prasad* magazine was born there in January 1963, along with Sandeepany Sadhanalaya. Some of the books began to

---

[2]   Refer *He Did It*, page 173, where it is reproduced from *Usha*, May 1961.

be published from there. Śrī Ram Batra, who was a pillar of support to the Mission in Mumbai, stocked the Mission publications at his office and sold them through his Bandbox laundry outlets. Later, the stocks were moved to the Mumbai āśrama, and Swami Premananda looked after the stocks and sale of books there.

▲ *Swami Premananda*

CHINMAYA PUBLICATIONS

FOR thousands of years, the wisdom contained in the scriptures written in Sanskrit, were available only to the priest class of India. In recent times Swami Chinmayananda is the singular force which has brought this knowledge into the homes of the Indian people.

Author of more than 30 scholarly works on the Bhagavad Geeta, the Upanishads and the Vedanta, he has been moving continuously across India and abroad, giving logical expositions in a language understandable to the modern educated man.

Swami Chinmayananda does not claim any personal theories or techniques. He teaches the highest philosophy of Vedanta, containing the basic Truths underlying all religions. He invites the questioning mind to protest against tradition, to scoff at empty ritual, to challenge idle dogmas, and to accept neither scripture nor Saint on hearsay.

In the United States, Swami Chinmayananda has been invited by major academic centres, including Harvard, Yale, Stanford, Berkeley, UCLA, New York University, Columbia, M.I.T., Boston College and many others throughout the country. Universities in Europe, Asia and the East, along with various institutions both here and abroad, have invited him to speak since his first departure from India in 1965.

As an orator, Swami Chinmayananda combines wit and brilliance. In India, his talks are attended daily by audiences of ten to twenty-five thousand. Giving a scientific basis to all his arguments, he is capable of reaching the minds and hearts of questioning seekers.

READ THE BOOKS OF CHINMAYA

The Hindu scriptures are famous for thoroughness, expression, clarity and logic and here the Swami brings them to us in the English language in their native beauty. The original Sanskrit verses with Roman transliteration accompanied by word meaning and followed by complete discourses on each verse is the method used in the commentaries.

There are hundreds of seekers who, without understanding the fundamentals, are aimlessly struggling along a vague spiritual path although they have behind them years of painstaking practices. The Swami's books take the trembling man by the hand to the heights of wisdom through such a gradient that he does not feel he is climbing a hill.

Outlined in the back of Kindle Life is a three-year 'Study Scheme', listing the order in which the books should be read and the daily portions to be studied. This plan systematically builds up, step by step, the fundamentals of Vedanta and provides a firm foundation for the student.

TEXT-BOOKS

KINDLE LIFE- A good book of introduction to the study of Vedanta. And in the Chinmaya 'Scheme of Study', this is the first book to be mastered. It contains discourses delivered by Swami Chinmayananda at various places. Price: 3-00

ATMA BODH- Employing the most beautiful similes and metaphors drawn from nature, the great teacher Sankara indicates the Vedantic thought. It is a most useful guide as an introduction to new students of Vedanta. Commentaries by Swami Chinmayananda. Price: 4-50

VIVEKACHUDAMANI- (Parts I & 2)- The Crest Jewel of Discrimination. This masterpiece of Sankara, clearly and brilliantly explained by Chinmaya, is the cream of the Upanishads and Bhagavad Geeta. As an introduction of Vedanta, it is one of the greatest text-books written. To one, who is making a deep study of Vivekachudamani, no other help is needed for leading him to a spiritual life and guiding him to his self-improvement. Price: 12-00

BHAJA GOVINDAM- In his exquisite poetry, Sankaraacharya indicates the Goal of Realization and describes the path to be taken. It also reveals the causes for the human misery and warns us of the consequences in continuing the present egocentric living. Price: 2-50

PLEASE WRITE TO:

CHINMAYA PUBLICATIONS TRUST
175, Rasappa Chetty Street Madras-600003.
Also available at all Mission Centres and Sandeepany Sadhanalaya Powai-Park-Drive, Bombay-400072.

▲ *This announcement appeared in* Tapovan Prasad *in May 1973.*

In the course of time, Śrī Parameshwar Namboodiri, who officiated as the temple priest, took charge of the book sales and dispatch at the Powai āśrama. In the early seventies, though many of the books were still being published from Chennai, some were brought out from centers like Delhi, Hyderabad, and Mumbai. The list of books advertised in a souvenir published at Bahrain in 1974 shows that publications were sourced from Chinmaya Publication Trust (Chennai), CCMT Publications (Mumbai), and Tapovan Kutir Publications (Uttarkashi). There seems to have been a period of overlap before operations were centralized in Mumbai in the late seventies.

C.P.T. PUBLICATIONS

English

Isavasyopanishad
Kenopanishad
Kathopanishad
Prasnopanishad
Mundakopanishad
Mandukya Karika
Taittiriyopanishad
Aithreyopanishad
Kaivalyopanishad
Atma Bodh
Bhaja Govindam
Meditation and Life
Kindle Life
Prayers Unto Him
Vedanta through Letters
Narada Bhakti Sutra
Bala Ramayanam
Geeta for Children
Vishnusahasranamam
Iswara Darsan
Radio Talks
Srimad Bhagavatham (by Cohen)
Wanderings in the Himalayas
Hail Renaissance Part I
—Do—   Part II
Ashtavakra Geeta
Geeta in 10 vols.) 1 Set
Geeta each vol.

Hindi

Isvasyopanishad
Prasanopanishad
Mundakopanishad
Mandukya Karika
Himagiri Vihar

Tamil

Isavasyopanishad
Kenopanishad
Kathopanishad
Bhaja Govindam
Medition and Life
Atma Bodh
Japayoga Gayatri
Geeta Text
—Do— (with meaning)

Malayalam

Isavasyopanishad
Kenopanishad
Kathopanishad
Atma Bodh
Bhaja Govindam
Meditation and Life
Iswara Darsan
Himagiri Vihar
Hindu mata rahasya
Geeta (with mean.)

Kannada

Aithreyopanishad
Bhaja Govindam

C.C.M.T. PUBLICATIONS

English

Geet (4 vols.) ordinary
—Do—   deluxe
Hymn to Dakshinamurty
Art of Living
Art of Meditation
Seek the Eternal
My Prayers — Part I
—Do—   — Part II
—Do—   — Part III
Vivekachoodamani Vol. I
—Do—   Vol. II
Tell Me a Story — Part I
—Do—   — Part II
We Must
With All Love and Om
Upadesa Saram
Dhyana Slokas
Immortality is your Birthright
On . . . Essay-lets
Moments with Krishna
Tune in the Mind
All Souvenirs
Secret of Action
The World, You and God
Can We

Hindi

Dharma Kathayem
Dhyan Aur Jeevan (Guj.)

Sindhi

Jeevan Jyothi Jagi

Marathi

Hindu dharma darsan

Miscellaneous

Aluminium Plaque — large
—Do—   — small

TAPOVAN KUTIR PUBLICATIONS

English

Purusha Sooktham
Bala Bhagavatham
Hasten Slowly
Hymn to Ganges
Hymn to Badrinath
Geeta Kilippattu
Soumyakasisastotram (text)
Soumyakasis with Commentary

Telugu

Kaivalyopanishad   ...
Hymn to Badrinath

Miscellaneous

Aluminium Plaque (Book Mark)
Swamiji's photo (Litho)

Śrī K. Sridhara Menon was in charge of the books section in the mid-seventies. Śrī C. M. Menon took over as manager of the book division from 1982 to 1991. His wife Subhadra was in charge of the kitchen store. She recalls, "Those nine years were the best time in our life. It was veritably heaven on earth. Gurudev's personal concern and support were unforgettable. I also had the good fortune to take care of Pūjya Guruji's[3] food; he was the Ācārya teaching the Vedānta Course then."

Some months after Śrī Menon left, Brni. Dhruti Chaitanya (now Swamini Nishchalananda) took charge of the Publication Division of CCMT in October 1991. She had just completed the Vedānta Course in Sidhbari under Swami Subodhananda and had come to Mumbai for the brahmacarya dīkṣā given by Pūjya Gurudev. She had joined the course at the age of thirty-eight and was eager to do intense sādhanā and engage in pracāra work to propagate the message of Vedānta.

▲ *Swamini Nischalananda with Pūjya Gurudev*

At that time, Śrī Narain Bhatia was looking after the book section along with other strenuous duties as an Assistant CEO. He put forth the proposal that Brni. Dhruti Chaitanya could take charge of the Publications Division. Her whirling thoughts resisted the idea. She was looking forward to working peacefully in the serene atmosphere of Sidhbari as indicated earlier by her Ācārya. When Pūjya Gurudev addressed the problem at the time of her dīkṣā in the Jagadeeshwara Temple, she was full of trepidation. He gauged her misgivings quickly and put her mind at rest by reassuring her, "You take care of my publications and I will look after your sādhanā!"

---

3 Swami Tejomayananda

What more could anyone ask for! However, face to face with the task, she realized that she knew next to nothing about printing and publication. Śrī Narain Bhatia was extremely helpful, briefing her on all aspects of her work and training her patiently. Let us hear the story in her own voice:

> In those days, there was no one in the book section except an accountant. We had to dispatch books regularly to every yajña venue as Gurudev moved from place to place. I had to pull out the heavy piles of books from where they were stacked, pack them, and mail them. There were times when I went to Śrī Bhatia for help because I could not reach the books stacked high up in the dark room. He would come personally, climb up rickety tables and shelves, for there were no ladders, and hand me the dusty piles of books.

▲ *Śrī Narain Bhatia and his wife Dr. Sarojini massage Pūjya Gurudev's feet.*

Slowly we started employing a few people to pack and do the heavy work. Ravi, who was already working in the kitchen, was one of the first to join the publications office; he works for CCMT even now. We began to check and clear the stocks systematically. In those days, when a book had to be reprinted, one of the old copies was simply handed over to the printer, who would do the rest. Gradually, we began to proofread the reprints.

By then, Swami Chidananda was teaching the Vedānta Course in Mumbai, and he helped a lot by proofreading the English books. Swami Advayananda was a student then, and he pitched in to transliterate the ślokas in *Vivekacūḍāmaṇi* and give the word meaning of the verses in English. Step by step, we began to improve the quality of the books. We introduced new covers, changing the monotonous single-colored covers with white lines and the title, which had become a standard with the printer. Mr. Puri was also a great help in all this.

Along with Śrī Bhatia, I had learned a little about the quality of paper and printing and wanted our books to be on par with international standards in appearance and quality. When I discussed this with Pūjya Gurudev, he rejected the proposal outright, because he wanted to keep the books affordable for the average reader.

Accounts had to be straightened out. There were outstanding amounts for the previous twenty years. Local yajña committees placed orders, and books were sent promptly; but there was no follow-up to get the payments. Slowly and painfully, many of the outstanding amounts were cleared, but some had to be written off. We put a proper system in place to send bills and make collections in time. Computerized billing was introduced. Catalogues were also updated and systematized.

At that time, only English and Gujarati books were published in Mumbai. Gujarati books were prepared in Ahmedabad and sent to Mumbai for printing. Books in other regional languages, like Telugu, Malayalam, Tamil, and Kannada, were published in the respective states. Hindi books were published from Kanpur and Marathi from Pune; both were moved to Mumbai in 1992.

Most of our books were then printed at Priya Graphics, and they still continue to publish some. The owner, Mr. Karunakaran, is a devotee, and in 1992, he had offered to hand over his printing press to Chinmaya Mission. Pūjya Gurudev blessed him by saying that the press and its owner were already his, but he did not want the Mission to have the added responsibility of running the press.

I was blessed by Pūjya Gurudev's Grace in abundance. He guided me in many subtle ways. I learned to listen to the voice of intuition and prevented many grave mistakes at the nick of the moment. Once when we were in the process of handing over the

Gujarati edition of *The Holy Geeta* to the printer, I casually turned the pages and the name of Narsi Mehta caught my attention. I did not know much Gujarati, but there it was! As I turned the pages, there were some more quotations of Narsi Mehta. I held the book back and we found that the editor had added those quotations in his innocent enthusiasm!

In another instance, after Pūjya Gurudev's Mahāsamādhi, we were told to send two copies of each book to be displayed in Gurudev's kuṭiyā in Sidhbari. I took out the books, instructed the packers, and returned to my room. After a little while, I felt restless. An inner voice kept nagging me to go and check. I resisted it for a while, but then relented and went to see what was happening. The packing was almost done, but the two sets of *The Holy Geeta* were smiling at me from a shelf nearby! *Gītā*, the very life and soul of Gurudev! Quickly the books went in.

Bhagavān Śrī Kṛṣṇa has promised in the *Gītā* to look after our yoga-kṣema, all our requirements, but with the condition that we have to remember Him constantly — ananyāścintayanto[4]. However, our Gurudev's compassion was such that, though I could not claim to have continual remembrance of the Lord, he took care of all my needs at work and in my personal life.

The work was very demanding. Every day I was in the office from 9:00 A.M. until almost 10:00 P.M. There was no time for sādhana or svādhyāya (self-study). Pūjya Guruji Swami Tejomayananda understood my plight and inducted Śrī K. C. Patnaik, who took over the responsibilities from the year 1995. The main reward of spending five years in publications was the stupendous increase in my faith and devotion to Pūjya Gurudev.

---

[4] *Bhagavad-gītā* 9.22

In the late eighties and early nineties, I used to print almost all the books except the *Holy Geeta*, which needed a special machine and extra-thin paper. All the books were paperbacks and printed in single color — even the front covers were plain and simple. Once, CCMT wanted me to print a hard-bound edition of *Vedanta Through Letters – Part 1*, and they requested me to hand the first copy of the book to Pūjya Gurudev. I still remember each and every word he said when I gave the book to him: "Nice book... nicely done... but I do not want such hard-bound books in the future. I want my books to be cheap, so that lots of people can buy and read them."

In 1992, when we had just started printing Gurudev's itinerary, a fire broke out and the press was engulfed in smoke. Quickly I told all the workers to come out and called for help. The fire raged on till evening and almost eleven to twelve fire engines arrived to put out the fire. Later on, I came to know that the fire had started in the adjacent Unit 128.

I called up Śrī Narain Bhatia and informed him immediately because many Mission books were in the press and Gurudev's itinerary had to be printed. To my surprise, the next day when I entered my Unit 127, except for a little water which had seeped inside, everything was intact! Unit 126, which belonged to a Maharashtrian fellow worker, who had great faith in Gurudev, was also miraculously saved.

Gurudev had been informed, but when he arrived in Mumbai, the itinerary was not ready. I stood on one side, tears welling up in my eyes. Gurudev called me to his side and roared, "Why are you crying when Lord Nārāyaṇa is with you! There is nothing to worry about." He then gave me a week's time to print the itinerary. He also queried, "Do you have insurance?" I did not have much hope in the insurance.

The Deputy Commissioner of Police, the Chief Fire Brigade Officer of Mumbai, and other officials who came to inspect the site, saw Gurudev's photo in my press and said, "That Baba only saved you!" The press was full of inflammable things like paper, kerosene, chemicals, and petrol. To my surprise, within a fortnight, I received a check for ₹4,25,000 from the insurance company — something unheard of. My loss was actually very meager. When Gurudev had remarked that Lord Nārāyaṇa is with you, it was indeed true, for He himself was Lord Nārāyaṇa!

– Śrī Karunakaran, Priya Graphics

Śrī K.C. Patnaik, who was a long-time devotee of Pūjya Gurudev and an active member of Chinmaya Mission from Rourkela, took charge of the Publication Division as general manager in July 1995. He gave a positive impetus to the sale of books all over the country, promoting Mission publications in bookshops, hotels, and prestigious clubs. He also toured extensively, meeting key persons in the various Mission centers, motivating them to increase the sales and teaching them the techniques of doing so.

▲ *Pūjya Gurudev with Śrī K.C. Patnaik*

Through the years, Pūjya Gurudev guided the publications department with his overall vision and, from time to time, also gave his suggestions regarding minute details. He used his tremendous marketing skills to promote the books as well. The personalized messages he wrote on the fly-leaf of the books for individual devotees sparkle with his special brand of wit and humor. In his parting gift of *The Holy Geeta* to Dr. Denton Cooley, who performed the by-pass surgery for him in 1980 at Houston, he wrote, "You saved my life, this may save yours."

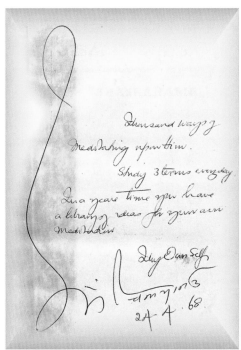

◄ *Message inscribed on a copy of*
Viṣṇu Sahasranāma

🎵 *Thousand ways of meditating upon Him.*

Study three terms every day. In a year's time, you have a library of ideas for your own meditation.

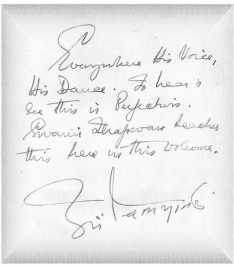

*Message on a book by
Swami Tapovan Maharaj* ►

🎵 *Everywhere His voice, His dance. To hear and see this is Perfection. Swami Tapovan teaches this here in this volume.*

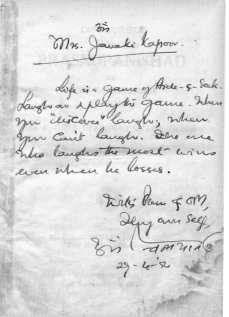

◄ *Message on a copy of*
The Holy Geeta

֎ *Five verses a day. Read,*
study, reflect. Thus do five
revisions of the entire Geeta.
What you understand, come to
live them. This is experiments
with Truth.

Profound advice on the
fly leaf of a book ►

֎ *Life is a game of hide*
and seek. Laugh on and
play the game. When you
"discover", laugh; when
you can't, laugh. The one
who laughs the most wins
even when he loses.

PART THREE

THE BRANCHES

The Branches

Chinmaya Publications West

Publication work in the West had its beginnings in 1966, during Swami Chinmayananda's second visit to the United States and the year he held the first yajña in the West, in the city of San Francisco, California. By 1973, the demand for his books had grown so much that the Chinmaya Study Group of Napa, which was handling the sales, found it difficult to manage the operation, and a separate unit named 'Chinmaya Books U.S.A.' was set up to handle the sales.

That same year, Gurudev had been invited to give talks at Esalen Institute in Big Sur, California. During a break between his talks,

Announcement

CHINMAYA BOOKS U.S.A., is the new name for the organization which is the sole distributor of books by Swami Chinmayananda, in the United States, Hawaii, Alaska and Canada.

Due to the increased volume of sales the Chinmaya Study Group of Napa will no longer be in charge of Chinmaya Books. This reorganizational move is intended to provide more efficiency and clarification of purpose.

Chinmaya Books U.S.A., is devoted solely to the stocking, distribution and promotion of books and book-sales in the above-mentioned territory. All book orders sent directly to India will be forwarded to this organization for processing.

Since Chinmaya Books U.S.A., is a totally non-profit organization, all money taken in above expenses is being kept in a fund to provide for Swamiji's spiritual work outside of India.

• Although the address will remain the same, all orders for books or records, should from this day be sent to :

CHINMAYA BOOKS U.S.A.

P. O. Box 2753

Napa, California 94558

▲ *Announcement published in* Tapovan Prasad, *May 1973*

Gurudev was conversing with some devotees from San Francisco. One of them, Rudite Emir, shyly told him that she was a professional editor and would be happy to offer her services, if he had need of them. He smiled and said, "No hurry. Time will tell."

And time did tell. A few years later, Gurudev asked Rudite to begin editing work on some existing Chinmaya texts. In 1975, among the first few texts he asked her to edit was *Wanderings in the Himalayas* by Swami Tapovanam, which was printed and published in India in 1977. Several other devotees, namely, Sheela Kripalani of New York and Winifred Schuetz of California, helped in the task by retyping the manuscripts. (In those days before the advent of computers, revising manuscripts was a labor-intensive task.) Among the early books was *Vedanta Concepts* (1984), a collection of short expositions of Vedāntic terms such as Om, avidyā, sannyāsa, vāsanā, and mokṣa. The definitions of these terms, in short, one-column expositions, had run in successive issues of *Mananam* (a quarterly publication during the early years). *Vedanta Concepts* was a compendium of those *Mananam* columns, and this book was also printed in the U. S. In addition, *Vedānta: A Self-Study*, a small booklet that used a programmed-learning approach to summarize key concepts of Vedānta, had been published under the authorship of Swami Chinmayananda and Rudite Emir by CCMT in 1985. Later books included *Śrī Rāma Gītā*, published by Chinmaya Publications West[1] and printed in the U.S. in 1986.

---

[1] Initially, Chinmaya Mission West (CMW) consisted of two organizations, CMW and Chinmaya Publications West (CPW). Robert Berg, Nalini Browning, Rudite Emir, and Rajendra Prasad were founding members of the CMW Board, and Nalini Browning, Rudite Emir, Leo Graves, and William Sheldon were founding members of the CPW Board. The first books published in the West were published by CPW; later, all publications came under the CMW banner.

Chinmaya Mission (West)
Fourth Report, August 30, 1975
Decatur, Georgia 30034, U.S.A.

Blessed One,
Hari Om! Hari Om! Hari Om!
Salutations!

Here I am again with my fourth report...

Both Chinmaya Mission (West) and Chinmaya Publication (West) have been incorporated in the State of California and they are now non-profit organizations recognized by the State Government. The CP(W) has already brought out a paperback book, *A Manual of Self-Unfoldment* ....

For all these activities, we will be needing funds. This initial fund is now to be raised by accepting 200 'Contributing Members' screened and recommended by the directors and finally accepted by Swamiji and confirmed by the CM(W) .... All 'Contributing Members' will receive (unless they default) all issues of *Mananam* and some of the books we publish each year ...

(Sd.) Swami Chinmayananda

In 1972, Gurudev had asked Bill Browning of Napa, California, to learn the printing trade, knowing full well that Browning would be playing a key role in printing not only books but also publicity materials and souvenirs for yajñas and camps. Among the camp souvenirs printed at Family Press by Bill Browning were handsome book-like publications titled *Preservation of Eternal Wisdom: The Work of*

Chinmaya Mission Around the World (1988) and *Resurgence of the Light: The Ageless Wisdom of India in the Modern Era* (1990). The Chinmaya Lesson Course was also revised, printed, and distributed by Nalini and Bill Browning in Napa, California, where the Family Press was first established.

During the early years of Chinmaya Mission West, Gurudev had made Nalini Browning in charge of distributing books within North America. The initial book distribution center was a small art-framing shop run by Leo Graves, who assisted Nalini with the book distribution. Indra Advani helped her to procure books from CCMT, Mumbai.

In 1981, the distribution center moved to Philadelphia, where the stocks were stored initially in the house of Surendra and Kusum Patel, and then in their store. From there, the stock of books was moved to Dipak Patel's home, and then to a public storage, and later to two trailers. These devotees also started Chinmaya Video Kendra for recording Gurudev's talks and making video copies under the leadership of Kusum Patel, Brni. Vilasini, Dr. AppaRao Mukkamala and Laju Bharucha.

In 1989, a biography of Swami Chinmayananda, *The Journey of a Master, Swami Chinmayananda: The Man, the Path, the Teaching*, authored by Nancy Patchen, was published by Asian Humanities Press in Berkeley, California, and was republished later by CCMT.

Other publishing projects included *Meditation and Life* (1992) and *Self-Unfoldment* (1992), both part of The Self-Discovery Series. Both books were edited by Rudite Emir and printed by Bill Browning of Family Press. *Self-Unfoldment* was a thoroughly revised and amended edition of *A Manual of Self-Unfoldment*, first published in Napa, California, by Chinmaya Publications West in 1975, with later reprints in India. Today, *Self-Unfoldment* has become a key introductory book for use in Study Groups. In 1993, *Hindu Culture: An Introduction*, based on lectures by Swami Tejomayananda, was published as part of The

Hindu Culture Series. *Hindu Culture* became a text used in local high schools as a resource of Indian studies in a fast-growing population of second-generation Indian students in California. In 2006, another book in The Hindu Culture Series was published: *Hinduism, Frequently Asked Questions*, based on Chinmaya Mission's earlier publication titled *Our Heritage* by R. S. Nathan (Swami Nityananda). The exhaustive revision was produced under the leadership of Brni. Aparna (now Swamini Akhilananda), with contributions by Rupali Gupta, Rudite Emir, Swami Advayananda, and the Chinmaya International Foundation (CIF).

On the East Coast, Raju Chidambaram undertook a significant publishing effort and compiled a thorough history of Chinmaya centers in the West. It was published as a camp souvenir in 1991 for the international camp in the state of Maryland.

Several small books on meditation were also revised and reprinted, such as *The Art of Meditation* (1990), revised with the help of editors Rudite Emir and Gail Larrick. After Gurudev's Mahāsamādhi in 1993, several publications saw the light of day, authored in the United States, but printed by CCMT in India. They include: *Swami Chinmayananda: A Life of Inspiration and Service* by Rudite Emir (1998, in anticipation of the celebration of 50 years of the Chinmaya Movement in 2001) and *At Every Breath, a Teaching: Stories About the Life and Teachings of Swami Chinmayananda,* also by Rudite Emir (1999).

In November 1992, new property was purchased at Langhorne, Pennsylvania, and Gurudev named it the Chinmaya Mission Tri-State Center, 'Kedar.' Publication activities moved to this new center and started functioning in a professional way under the leadership of Surendra Patel and Kusum Patel.

Gurudev saw the growth of the publications effort and, in 1993, assigned Swami Siddhananda to be in charge of Chinmaya Publications

West. Since then, Swami Siddhananda has made a remarkable contribution to the marketing of Chinmaya literature in the West. Today there is a catalog of more than 450 books, 150 CDs, 100 DVDs, and 100 gift items. Most of the orders are received online through the website, locally as well as internationally. Dedicated volunteers at every Chinmaya Mission center order these items and take care of the sales, stock, and accounts. Orders are received not only from individuals, but also other organizations, temples, churches, libraries and bookstores.

Regional Publications in India

Hindi

Pūjya Gurudev conducted his first Delhi yajña in the last quarter of 1953. It was received with great enthusiasm, and soon there was a demand for Hindi translations of the *Yagna Prasad*. In 1954, Smt. Sheela Sharma started translating into Hindi Swamiji's talks on the *Kaṭhopaniṣad* from his first jñāna yajña in Poona. It was completed by February 1955 and was printed by the Agra University Press. Gurudev guided her through a series of letters that are now preserved in the archives department of CCMT in Mumbai. In one of the letters in 1954, he writes:

> Please take your own time for the translation; there is no hurry. I hope it will be completely ready by the time I come over to Delhi in Feb. Of course, you will have to see the proof yourself, and the printer is to be arranged with your help, but by me. The cover page you may change, but the "Torch" in some form or other must be there. It is the insignia of the *Yagna* books. The selling part of it I may or may not give your man — since I feel that direct dealing with the customers is more advisable for my work. I want to know who are all the enthusiasts — and they

Please take your own time for the translation; there is no hurry. I hope it will be completely ready by the time I come over to Delhi in Feb. Of course you will have to see the proof yourself, and the printer is to be arranged with your help, but by me. The cover page you may change; but the "Torch" in some form or other must be there. It is the ensignia of the Yagna-books. The

Selling part of it I may or may not give to you when ___ suffice I feel that direct dealing with the customers is more advisable for my work. I want to know who are all the enthusiasts ___ and they must be by letter contacted; by literature - freely fed from time to time. This is not possible if sales are arranged through a sole-agent; though the book will get well advertised, no doubt. We will discuss this when we meet!!

Certainly I want to write the preface with your thick and living all about it. Both I can write again in English! See I had already done a bit of it on the cover page of Yagna Prasad No V. or IV. recently issued from Delhi! You please give me a rough draft & I shall do the rest ___ I am new to press: remember there are a 2000 - 3000 burning, scathing crowd to be fed & a new book to be thought out, written, proof-read, & published, all in these 101 days.. And my Sheelas and Sushielas demanding sewas.!!

must be by letter contacted, by literature freely fed from time to time. This is not possible if sales are arranged through a sole agent, though the book will get well advertised, no doubt. We will discuss this when we meet!!

Certainly I want to write the preface ... But I can write only in English! See I had already done a bit of it on the cover page of *Yagna Prasad* No. V or IV recently issued from Delhi! You please give me a rough draft and I shall do the rest — I am now too pressed: remember, there is a 2000–3000 burning, seething crowd to be fed and a new book to be thought out, written, proofread, and published — all in these 41 days!! And my Shielas and Sushielas[2] demanding sewas!!

▲ *Sheela Sharma with Pūjya Gurudev*

---

[2] In the letters, Swamiji addresses Sheela Sharma as 'Sushiela Sharma,' and Shiela refers to Shiela Puri, who published many of the books from Delhi.

In another letter, dated March 10, 1955, Gurudev writes to her: "How sweet of you to think of and start the translation work of *Īśāvāsya*. I have no words to express my gratitude."

In the meantime, someone else had translated the book *Meditation and Life* and the booklet *Creative Power*, based on the talks given to the students of Poona University. Gurudev's talks on *Māṇḍūkya Upaniṣad* and *Kārikā* were translated into Hindi and published by Shiela Puri in 1957. The *Praśnopaniṣad* discourses in Madurai were the next to come out in book form in Hindi. *Geeta for Children* was translated as *Bal Geeta* by Śrī B.C. Pandey. All these books were printed by Kapur Printing Press and Gulab Printing Press in Delhi.

Gurudev's first jñāna yajña in Kanpur, held in 1967, gave further impetus to the publishing work in Hindi. The interest generated by the discourses on the *Gītā* (chapter 3) and *Bhaja Govindam* left the people thirsting for more. In the previous ten years, many new books and commentaries by Gurudev had appeared in English, and the Hindi-speaking seekers wanted to read them in their own language.

Śrī Pratap Chandra Shukla (later known as Swami Shankarananda) took the lead in Hindi publications in Kanpur. He was already publishing a weekly news bulletin called 'Civic Service.' Śrī Shukla started translating *Kindle Life* into Hindi and published it in the news bulletin as a series. On its completion, he sought and received permission from Swamiji to publish it as a book. Thus the Hindi Publication Division was started in the year 1980, and the first book, *Jīvan Jyoti*, a translation of *Kindle Life*, was published under the banner of 'Chinmaya Hindi

▲ *Swami Shankarananda*

Sahitya.' The news bulletin 'Civic Service' was converted into a full-fledged Hindi journal called *Chinmaya Chandrika*, which continues to cater to the Hindi-speaking population in India.

At the age of seventy, Swami Shankarananda learned to use the computer and started doing the full layout of 'Chinmaya Chandrika' at Mandhana āśrama. He trained one of the village boys from his Yuva Kendra group to type in Hindi and gave him a keyboard on which Hindi alphabets were pasted. This boy, named Suresh, proved to be an asset for Swamiji.

The electric supply to the āśrama was erratic in those days — six hours in the daytime for a week and six hours in the night during the next week. Swamiji would work with his boys from 3:30 in the morning until 5:00 A.M., when the electricity was shut off. And from 7:00 A.M., Swamiji used to give lectures on the *Gītā* or the *Rāmāyaṇa*. All through his busy schedule the whole day, he would remain smiling. And the 'Chinmaya Chandrika' always came out on time.

Swamiji wrote many books. Even while writing, if someone came with a problem, Swamiji would take time to talk with him and help him out. And as soon as the person left the room, Swamiji would continue with his writing. In spite of this, his handwritten manuscripts were clean, with no cutting or overwriting.

In the year-end issue of 'Chinmaya Chandrika,' Swamiji always featured a book — a translation of Pūjya Gurudev's work, or his own commentary on one of Ādi Śaṅkara's compositions, or his own book.

– Manju Tyagi

In 1976, Br. Vivek Chaitanya (now Swami Tejomayananda, head of Chinmaya Mission Worldwide), was posted to Kanpur. He stayed there for four years and contributed in a big way to the expansion of Chinmaya Hindi Sahitya. His Hindi translation of *The Holy Geeta* marked a major milestone in Hindi publications. Smt. Nirmala Bajoria, who was the president of the Kanpur chapter of Chinmaya Mission at that time, sponsored the Hindi *Gītā* in memory of her late husband Śrī Banwari Lal Bajoria. In fact, it was she who requested the translation, encouraged it, and provided all logistical support. The first edition of 500 copies, priced at ₹ 40 each, was soon sold out.

When I started translating *The Holy Geeta* in Hindi, I felt that the language should be very simple. After translating the first few pages, I showed it to an expert in Hindi literature, who was well-versed in English also, for his comments and suggestions. After all, Hindi is not my mother tongue, and this was the first time I had tried my hand at translation. He said, "If you are writing your own book, then you can use the language you want. But if you are translating, your language should correspond to the original. Here, the original is in high-flown language with beautiful expressions, so the Hindi translation should also be of the same quality. The translation should be true to the original." He also pointed out a particular mistake in sentence construction that occurred repeatedly in my translation. Once I understood and corrected that, it was a smooth flow. There were no rough copies, fair copies, or typed copies. The book was printed directly from my manuscript. This is called grace.

How did the grace come about? Initially, when I thought of translating *The Holy Geeta*, it seemed very intimidating. Every day, I would pick up the book, and then looking at its size, put it away again. It was a good 1,000 pages! Soon, a thought occurred to me: I should write to Gurudev that I am taking up this translation work and ask for his blessings. It would help in two ways. First, he would send his blessings. Second, he would inquire about its progress from time to time. That would push me to do the work.

And sure enough, within six months, the translation was completed. I worked eight hours a day. I stayed put in Kanpur for a whole month to do this. One day, when I was writing in their house, Mrs. Bajoria, who sponsored the book, came and stood behind me quietly. When I became aware of it, I turned around, and she said, "You know why I am working? Because I can't do what you are doing!" She was the executive director of a woolen mill.

Apart from that one month in Kanpur, I was traveling, conducting yajñas, giving lectures in the mornings and evenings. Thus, some chapters were written in Kanpur and others in Rewa, Kolkata, and other places. But I concluded it only in Kanpur.

▶

> I can never forget that night. I went on writing, and there were still 4–5 pages more to be completed, but I was tired and went to bed. But I could not sleep. Something within was waking me up and goading me to get up and write. And I did. The security guard in that big house must have wondered why the light in my room was on all night. Early morning, around four o'clock, I wrote the last page. I had thought that when the work was completed, I would scream in joy and excitement. But what happened was just the opposite. There was utter silence. It was such a nice feeling. I can never forget that last night and the sense of bliss on completion.
>
> – Swami Tejomayananda

Br. Vivek Chaitanya conducted many jñāna yajñas during his stay in Kanpur. Some of the texts chosen did not have Hindi translations of the commentaries, so the work was hastened in order to bring out the books in time for the jñāna yajñas. All along, Gurudev kept guiding him. In a letter dated March 8, 1980, he writes, "Do not try literal translation. The ideas must come in the same sequence, but do not try to translate from English directly into Hindi; then the native beauty of Hindi will be lost." In the words of Pūjya Guruji, "It was to be a translation of thoughts."

Pūjya Guruji recalls: "When the Hindi Publication Division was set up, Gurudev had told me three things: You should get some books translated, find sponsors to bring them out in print, and you must also translate some. The third was a difficult one. But by his Grace, I fulfilled all three tasks. I translated *Muṇḍakopaniṣad* and *Īśāvāsya Upaniṣad*, besides *The Holy Geeta*. And I got the *Kaṭhopaniṣad* translated by Deepa Modi. Her family sponsored it, too."

Some of the texts on which Br. Vivek Chaitanya spoke were not available in book form in Chinmaya Mission at that time. The first one of these was *Dṛg-Dṛśya-Viveka*. In the preface to the commentary on this text published later, he writes:

> In June 1977, the Kanpur Chinmaya Mission center organized a jñāna yajña in which I gave daily morning discourses on Bhagavan Śaṅkarācārya's Vedāntic scripture *Dṛg-Dṛśya-Viveka*. At that time I had no inclination to write a commentary on it, but Śrī Pratap Chandra Shukla (Pūjya Swami Shankarananda in sannyāsa āśrama), who was a very diligent member of Kanpur Chinmaya Mission and also had deep Vedāntic knowledge, recorded these lectures and transcribed them. I am grateful to Śrī Shukla for the work he has done in the publication of this book.

The next original commentary by Br. Vivek Chaitanya to come out was on Śrī Ramana Maharshi's *Upadeśa Sāra*. One of the brahmacārīs recorded the talks and transcribed them. In the preface to this book, Br. Vivek Chaitanya writes: "The credit for getting this commentary by me in the written form goes to the members of the Chinmaya Mission Lucknow center, and the credit for getting it published goes to the Kanpur center."

The office of the Hindi publications functioned at Vivek Press, Brahm Nagar. Śrī Shukla received sannyāsa dīkṣā in 1986 and moved to Mandhana, where the construction of the new āśrama had begun. By that time, twenty-four Hindi books had been published, and the remaining stock was moved to Mandhana.

In the next few years, many more books were translated and published in

Hindi. Swami Shankarananda was a prolific writer and authored many commentaries and original books, besides translating and publishing the books of Pūjya Gurudev. His detailed commentary on *Pañcadaśī* has been published in four volumes by CCMT. The two books he wrote for senior citizens are a major contribution to the literature for Central Chinmaya Vanaprastha Sansthan. His involvement was such that his name became synonymous with Chinmaya Hindi Publications.

Some of the other people who made a significant contribution to the translation work in Hindi were Śrī K.L. Kharbandha, Śrī Om Prakash Batra, Smt. Shanti Gurha, Smt. Shail Mehrotra, Swamini Geetananda, Swami Bhaskarananda, Swamini Amitananda, Dr. Vishwanath Mishra, and Smt. Manju Tyagi. This list is by no means exhaustive. Smt. Shakuntala Varma (later known as Brni. Shanti Chaitanya and then Swamini Samvidananda) undertook the mammoth task of translating Pūjya Gurudev's commentary on *Vivekacūḍāmaṇi*, which was then published in two volumes in 1992. She also translated some Marathi books of Swami Purushottamananda, and so did Sushri Vanamala Gore, Śrī Anant Kaitwade, and Śrī Pradeep Nayak.

Some of the most popular titles are *Mānas ke Motī* in three volumes, compiled from Swami Subodhananda's talks on *Rāmacaritmānas*, and *Śrīmad Bhāgavata*, talks of Swami Tejomayananda, compiled by Swamini Amitananda.

In 1992, the Hindi publications moved to Mumbai, under the wing of the CCMT Publications Division. It continues to flourish with an ever-expanding circle of readers.

Marathi

Pūjya Gurudev recognized the divine potential in one of his earliest disciples, Br. Purushottam Chaitanya, who was to become the revered Swami Purushottamananda in later years. Gurudev put him in charge of the state of Maharashtra. Following the footsteps of his master, Br. Purushottam began to conduct jñāna yajñas in Marathi, traveling indefatigably all over the

state. Naturally, the need arose for texts in Marathi. Devotees were encouraged to translate the commentaries of Pūjya Gurudev and other books already published by Chinmaya Mission. As per available records, the first Marathi book titled *Hindu Dharma Darśan* was published in October 1968.

The Marathi translation committee was officially formed at Pune in January 1981. Translation of the individual chapters of Gurudev's commentary on *Bhagavad-gītā* began around this time. The first Marathi book published from Chinmaya Mission Pune was the commentary on *Gaṇapati Atharvaśīrṣa*, written by S.G. Savarkar, an ardent devotee of Pūjya Gurudev. Slowly, the commentaries on *Ātma Bodha, Bhaja Govindam, Dakṣiṇāmūrti Stotram*, and the various Upaniṣads were translated into Marathi.

Śrī Rambhau Telang was the first president of the Marathi translation committee. Sarvashri Samsare, Śrī Bavdhane, Śrī V. L. Deshpande, Śrī Bhai Naidu, Śrī Ratnaparakhi, Smt. Veena Pendase, Smt. Sunita Bavale, and Smt. Shalinitai Marathe were among the team members. Many other devotees offered technical assistance by proofreading and maintaining records and accounts.

In the course of time, the work slowed down and almost stopped. In 2005, Swami Purushottamananda entrusted the translation work to the Chinmaya Prakashan Marathi Vibhag, headed by Ācārya Varsha of Chinmaya Mission Dombivli. This committee includes Ācārya Vivek, Brni. Sandhya Chaitanya, Smt. Savita Chakravarty, and Śrī Sudhakar Hampihallikar. Many new books have been brought out under their supervision.

▲ *Swami Purushottamananda*

Among them are Swami Purushottamananda's commentaries on *Kaivalyopaniṣad, Nārāyaṇa Sūktam, Cāṅgdev Pāsaṣṭī*, and *Sadācāra*.

Gujarati

The earliest books in Gujarati were translations of the smaller books like *Sādhana Pañcakam* with Gurudev's commentary. Śrī Y. T. Tarkas translated many books with untiring enthusiasm. In a letter dated August 12, 1980, Pūjya Gurudev indicates the order in which he was to take up the books for translation: "It is extremely gratifying to note that you have taken up now for translation, *I Love You* booklet .... Thereafter, as you say, you can take up *Hasten Slowly, We Must, Vedānta Through Letters, Self-Unfoldment, Man-Making*, etc." Br. Swaroop Chaitanya[3] was in charge of Gujarati publications at that time.

---

[3] No longer with Chinmaya Mission.

In 1986, Brni. Smriti Chaitanya (now Swamini Vimalananda) was posted to Ahmedabad. Her dynamic presence inspired a spurt in the publication work in Gujarati. With her initiative, it was decided to publish Gujarati translations of Gurudev's commentaries on the Upaniṣads in the form of souvenirs during the major jñāna yajñas. This served the dual purpose of raising funds through advertisements and making Gurudev's books available in the local language. Thus, books were translated year after year, and almost all the Upaniṣad commentaries were made available in Gujarati. Sometimes, reprints of

▲ *Page two of Pūjya Gurudev's letter dated June 23, 1986, to Brni. Smriti Chaitanya with advice about translations*

The attempt at translation will steady your mind, and while translating, keep your readers in mind. Consider them as absolute novices, and so try to explain everything, even what Tejo (Swami Tejomayananda) has explained. Make it most useful.

books were also undertaken in the same way. Śrī Yogeshbhai Desai and Śrī Y. T. Tarkas made major contributions in translating these books.

This method of publishing translations as souvenirs was emulated in Vadodara also. Later, when Swamini Vimalananda moved to Coimbatore, the same work was done by translating books into Tamil, the native language of the state.

Swamini Krishnapriyananda, Swami Deveshananda, and Br. Atharvana Chaitanya are carrying on the good work. Since most of the Gujarati people understand Hindi as well, the demand for Gujarati books is not a pressing need. Hindi books sell well in the region.

Telugu

In 1979, Gurudev asked the then president of Chinmaya Mission Proddatur, Śrī J. Vemaiah, to start the Telugu Division of CCMT Publications, and since then, Telugu translations of Gurudev's commentaries began to be published from Proddatur. The Telugu translation of *The Holy Geeta* was released by Gurudev in Cochin in 1980. It ran through two editions of 2,000 copies each. Almost thirty titles were thus translated into Telugu and went through many editions in the next decade.

◄ A page from Gurudev's letter to Smt. Lakshmi Reddy, dated November 19, 1975

We want to have all the 3–4 Telugu books published by May each 1500-2000 copies each. Give them to 2 or 3 presses. VRVS will be able to organise it. Let him take the responsibility. You line up the proofreaders. We need 3–4 different proofreaders, each responsible for each book.

Let me have the estimate 1. Paper 2. Printing 3. Gathering 4. Stitching 5. Binding — for each book separately.

Then contact Sivasankar Reddy. See if we can get paper required from Andhra Paper through (the) manager, who is Reddy's tenant. VRVS can give an estimate of paper needed for 4 books in crown — 1/16 size.

Swamini Saradapriyananda, Smt. T. Annapoorna, and Smt. Vijaya Murthy were among those who translated the books. In those days, the main person who was conducting jñāna yajñas in Telugu

▲ *Pūjya Gurudev releases Swamini Sarada-priyananda's Telugu commentary on the Gītā. Śrī Vijaya Saradhi receives a copy from Gurudev.*

and propagating the message of the *Gītā* and the Upaniṣads in the true tradition of Chinmaya Mission was Swamini Saradapriyananda, who had studied in the very first batch of Sandeepany Sadhanalaya under Gurudev in the early sixties. Known for her intense austerity and passionate espousal of the teachings of Vedānta, she wanted books to be made available to everyone at affordable prices. Besides the major Upaniṣads for which commentaries were available, she taught many rare Upaniṣads for which the texts were not available. And texts were essential for the listeners to follow the talks, chant the verses, and study them on their own after the talks. The people of the small towns and villages where she gave talks could not afford to spend much on books. Hence was born the idea of Chinmayaranyam Publication Trust.

Gurudev was happy with the publication trust proposal, and, with his permission, the trust began to function from Guntur in 1987. Śrī G. Vijaya Saradhi[4] dedicated himself to the work wholeheartedly. He sourced paper in bulk from wholesale dealers at nominal prices, visited the press every day, and personally proofread and corrected

---

4   Father of Brni. Prarthana Chaitanya

mistakes, leaving no stone unturned to make the books available at the lowest cost for the people at large. Book after book rolled out — commentaries by Swamini Saradapriyananda on *Vajrasūti Upaniṣad*, *Sūryopaniṣad*, *Bhāvanopaniṣad*, *Īśāvāsyopaniṣad*, and many others, including the *Bhagavad-gītā*.

> Gurudev conducted a jñāna yajña in Guntur in 1989. At the end of the yajña, he was told about the brisk sale of books at the venue. The newly printed copies of the commentary on the *Gītā* by Swamini Saradapriyananda had sold like hot cakes. Swamiji asked how many copies of *The Holy Geeta* with his own commentary in English had been sold. "Two or three" came the reply from someone. "Never mind, that is for an international audience; this is the local need," remarked Swamiji.
>
> – Śrī Vijaya Saradhi

For more than a decade, Śrī Vijaya Saradhi functioned as the right hand of Swamini Saradapriyananda in publishing books. The inventory was stored in his house; the trust functioned from there and

▲ *The first meeting of Chinmayaranyam Publication committee with Swamini Saradapriyananda. Śrī Vijaya Saradhi is seated on the extreme right, next to Swamini.*

a room was set apart for Swaminiji to stay and work there whenever she wanted. However, problems in his personal life snowballed and he had to resign in 1999.

By the late 1990s, the advent of computers had started changing the processes of layout and printing. Swamini Saradapriyananda was one of the first to acquire and start using a personal computer in Chinmayaranyam, Ellayapalle. In 1997, she called over Tukaram, one of the students to whom she had taught Vedānta, to help her with the publications. She taught him the art of typing and the basics of a computer. He was a natural at it and learned a lot on his own. He began to do the layout and cover designs in consultation with Swamini Saradapriyananda, and later with Swamini Seelananda. To this day, he has designed 90 percent of the books published by the trust.

As the Chinmayaranyam Publication Trust flourished, the Telugu Publication Division of CCMT, which was managed by Śrī Vemaiah, was merged with it in 1997. Bhimavaram became the headquarters for the trust; books were stocked there, though the actual printing continued to be done from Vijayawada and other places.

Swamini Saradapriyananda was very keen to have an in-house printing press. The idea of a press in the Guntur Chinmaya Vidyalaya premises had been mooted. Gurudev shot it down saying, "I do not want my children to be exposed to the sounds of machines and the bickering of a labor union!"

Swamini Saradapriyananda translated Pūjya Gurudev's commentary on *The Holy Geeta* in her last days. When her deteriorating health made it impossible for her to write or type anymore, she started dictating and recording the translation. These recordings are now being transcribed, and the process of bringing out this version of the Telugu translation of the classic commentary by Gurudev is well on the way. Swamini Seelananda has already prepared the first three chapters for publication.

For many years, the stock and sales of books at Bhimavaram have been managed by Śrī Ramachandra Murti. His sister, B. Pravaramba, who attended the Vedānta Course, handles the translations of many books from English to Telugu, along with Smt. Vijaya Murthy and Śrī T. Janardhan. So far, thirty-six books of Pūjya Gurudev and eighteen books by Pūjya Swami Tejomayananda have been translated. Other popular titles like *At Every Breath, a Teaching* and *Why Do We* are also available in Telugu.

Malayalam

Pūjya Gurudev's fourth jñāna yajña was conducted in Palakkad in January 1954. With that arose the need for Malayalam translations of books. This was done by various devotees as and when needed. Gurudev's letter dated May 11, 1955, to his cousin Bhaskara Menon, shows the urgency of getting the Malayalam translations done in time for their use in the jñāna yajñas:

Please meet Dr. Vasudevan. That day we met, at the Arumula Ashram, a man (Editor of *Desabandhu* or so) who was anxious to translate our books. Please contact him and see if he can immediately translate for me ISA.[5] If so, please request him to translate it in a month's time — we can get it printed in *Matrubhumi* as usual and use them in Trivandrum.

If it is not convenient for him to do so, then contact Achari of Ernakulam High School and see if he can. If he also fails, then consult Padmanabha Nair (Krishnan Nair Bros) and Krishna Pillai.

We want the translation in a month's time — by June 20th — free translation — no rights for the translator — a work-of-love dedicated to the great mission of ours.

In case we get the translation, we undertake to get it printed before the Travancore yagna.

REMIT Rs. 3/- for YAGNA and get your copy of
DISCOURSES ON MUNDAKOPANISHAD.

---

[5] *Īśāvāsyopaniṣad*

Janaki Menon was one of the main translators and her house, 'Parvati Niwas, Diwan's Road, Ernakulam – 16' was the official address of Chinmaya Mission Ernakulam until the mid-seventies. In the 1950s, along with her sister Meena Haridas, she translated Gurudev's commentaries on the first 100 verses of *Vivekacūḍāmaṇi*, as also *Īśāvāsyopaniṣad* and *Bhaja Govindam*.

Another well-known address was that of Damodara Menon, who was a graduate in literature, and who served as editor of *Tapovan Prasad* in the mid-seventies. He translated Gurudev's commentaries on *Nārada Bhakti Sūtram*, *Viṣṇu Sahasranāmam*, *Hymn to Ganga*, and *Saumyakāśīśa Stotram* in his later years. Till the mid-sixties, Chinmaya Mission Calicut functioned from his residence — Vengalil House, Chalappuram, Calicut – 2.

By the late seventies, there was a deeply felt need to organize the Malayalam Publications in a systematic way. In the course of time, a center for this was established in Koduvally, Calicut, and Śrī Gopalan was put in charge of it. He was assisted by Śrī Damodara Menon. It is interesting to see how Gurudev guided the entire process in a letter dated March 30, 1983, addressed to Śrī Sukumaran, advocate, Palakkad, giving detailed instructions:

> Jai Jai Jagadeeswara! Salutations!!
> I have been watching the progress of our publication (Malayalam) and I would like to draw your personal attention to it.
>
> Each center and sevak must feel that publications are an integral part of our Jñāna Yajñas. Its smooth, successful functioning is each one's responsibility. Just for convenience, we have selected Koduvally–Kozhikode as its headquarters and Gopalan as its in-charge.

Individuals and the institutions are welcome to patronize publication by donating the cost of publishing a book — ₹ 15,000 — either in the loving memory of one's beloved one, living or departed, or on your own behalf.

Each center will come forward to publish at least one book. If any center feels that it cannot afford to donate the amount, efforts should be made to find a donor for this.

We note with gratitude the generous donations of the following individuals and institutions at this altar:

Sri K. S. Viswanathan of Trichy (who donated for publishing *Bhagavad Geeta — Swadhyayam* in loving memory of his late son: Raju).

Dr. (Mrs.) Yashoda Raghavan of Kasargod (for *Bala Vihar Bhajanavali* – 3rd edition).

Chinmaya Mission College, Taliparamba (for *Bhaja Govindam* new edition).

Chinmaya Mission, Kozhikode (for *Kindle Life — Jeevitham Dhanyamakkan* – 2nd edition).

Hereafter, when a script is ready, our publication department will prepare an estimate for printing 3,000 copies.

Our major centers in Kerala (Cannanore, Kozhikode, Palghat, Trichur, Ernakulam, Trivandrum, etc.) will immediately place orders for at least 200 copies with payment in advance. CCMT also will give advance for 1,000 copies. Gopalan will intimate the cost to you and CCMT. You remit the amount by demand draft drawn in favor of: CCMT — Chinmaya Publications (Malayalam Division) — payable at Calicut. This will enable us to meet the initial expenses of the press, and so we can ask the press to start printing immediately. This will further help the publication division in many ways:

Piling up of stock at the headquarters can be avoided.

Each center (which makes the advance payment) will naturally be compelled to attend to its sale.

Unnecessary clerical work at the headquarters, such as keeping the accounts, sending reminders to centers to send the accounts, etc., can be reduced.

Old accounts — outstanding dues may be settled immediately. Send the accounts promptly at least once in two months. Don't wait for reminders from Gopalan. He has other work also — prachar work in interior villages. He writes to you not on his own accord. He consults with me in all matters and only on getting my approval, he contacts you. So when he writes to you, please respond. I note that some centers are not very regular in sending the accounts to him. Trichur is very prompt — I appreciate it. Trivandrum sends the accounts when reminded. But there are a few centers whose attitude seems to be intolerably irresponsible. This is very unfair and should not happen hereafter.

I am closely watching the progress. Please cooperate.

With Prem and Om,
Thy Own Self,
– Chinmaya

This letter shows how Gurudev kept a tight control over things, noticed small details, gave hints about systems and processes, appreciated good workers, acknowledged donations, kept track of finances, encouraged sponsorships, and made it clear that he was aware of all that was happening so that defaulters would be put on the alert. All this and much more in a single stroke, a single letter!

Kalyani Kutty Amma, mother of Śrī Vasudevan[6], who hosted Gurudev during his sojourns in Jamshedpur, translated *Tell Me a Story* into Malayalam. Gurudev used to call her Annapoorneshwari, as she would feed 600 delegates at a time during the yajñas in Jamshedpur.

All along, Ācārya Atma Chaitanya, who had studied the Vedānta Course at Sandeepany Sadhanalaya in the early seventies and had then dedicated himself to serve Pūjya Gurudev, was involved in the Malayalam Publications. On August 18, 1976, much before the activities were centralized in Koduvally, Gurudev wrote to him, "I will send you the list of Malayalam translations so that the office there will have the record of all the translations done already. You will keep on making it up-to-date. A. S. Menon is arranging for the translation of the *Manual of Self-Unfoldment*." Later, the *Manual* was translated by Sugatha Kumari, who titled it *Ātma Vikāsam*.

Gurudev continues in that letter, "When the list is complete with us, always up-to-date, if there is any enquiry from anyone, we can always advise them properly, that either the translation has already been done or is being done, or the translator would be doing a great service by taking up this work.

"Some of the chapters of the *Bhagavad Geeta* were done by Paru Kutty. You may enquire with her where the manuscripts are. Please collect the manuscript as far as it has been done. The rest we can get translated in the same spirit as Paru Kutty's translation."

---

6   Son-in-law of Gurudev's cousin, Śrī Bhaskara Menon

The Holy Geeta was translated in bits and pieces by various people whenever necessary. Later these were discarded when the final translation was done by Gopalan, Damodaran, and Krishnan Kutty Kurup. Gopalan also translated *Vivekacūḍāmaṇi, Muṇḍakopaniṣad, Bhaja Govindam, Kindle Life, God Symbolism, Sādhana Pañcakam*, and *Śrī Rāma Gītā. Ātma Bodha* was translated by Krishnan Kutty Kurup.

On September 8, 1976, Gurudev writes from Tapovan Kuti to Ācārya Atma Chaitanya:

> I am glad to find that about 16 books of ours have been already translated into Malayalam and many of them are available ....
>
> You will kindly write to Sri Govinddas Parekh and come to know through him the stock position of Malayalam books and order them from him. You can take these books to the various centers where you are having your yagnas ....
>
> You can ask Advocate Karunakaran of Calicut to translate any of the books that have not yet been translated if he can do it for the popular concern and not for literary men. Our attempt is missionary work and therefore we must have our books in a very simple and humble language. The translation will be entirely ours and the translator will have no rights at all.

In another letter, dated April 2, 1984, he tells Atma Chaitanya to take the printers to task:

> Change the printers. They are not using ink, but leftover water after washing old bottles of ink. This is so dirty and so dim that all the publicity value of the folder is lost. It must be at least five times clearer.

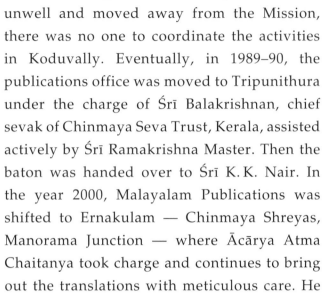

In the late eighties, when Gopalan became unwell and moved away from the Mission, there was no one to coordinate the activities in Koduvally. Eventually, in 1989–90, the publications office was moved to Tripunithura under the charge of Śrī Balakrishnan, chief sevak of Chinmaya Seva Trust, Kerala, assisted actively by Śrī Ramakrishna Master. Then the baton was handed over to Śrī K. K. Nair. In the year 2000, Malayalam Publications was shifted to Ernakulam — Chinmaya Shreyas, Manorama Junction — where Ācārya Atma Chaitanya took charge and continues to bring out the translations with meticulous care. He

has translated the commentaries on *Badarīśa Stotram, Manīṣā Pañcakam,* and *Puruṣa Sūktam,* among other books. Sunanda Gopalakrishnan assists him in the editing and proofing work. Swami Gabheerananda, who is well-versed in both Malayalam and Sanskrit, has helped out readily in times of need.

In recent years, Pūjya Swami Tejomayananda's *Bhāgavata Pravacan* has been translated by I. K. Master, *Dakṣiṇāmūrti Stotram* and *Aitareya Upaniṣad* by P. Krishnan Master, and *Kaivalya Upaniṣad* by Girija Bai. There are more than thirty books available in Malayalam now. Malayalam versions of yajña prasāda booklets like *Why Study Gītā, Rishiproktam,* and *Call of the Sages* are used extensively during the local yajñas.

Tamil

Madras (now Chennai) was one of the first few venues where Pūjya Gurudev conducted jñāna yajñas. The talks were in English and most of the listeners could read English very well. However, as the movement gathered strength, the local populace demanded books in Tamil. *Kaṭhopaniṣad, Ātma Bodha, Bhaja Govindam* and *Meditation and Life* were some of the earliest books translated by Śrī T. Seshadri of Madurai. The first volume of the *Bala Vihar Guide Book* in Tamil was released in October 1969.

Tamil translations of Gurudev's articles and books appeared periodically from the very early years, but the Tamil Publications Division of CCMT was started only in September 1982. The first major task undertaken was the translation of Pūjya Gurudev's

▲ *Announcement published in the November 1969 issue of* Tapovan Prasad

commentary on the *Bhagavad-gītā*. Śrī C. G. Vasudevan, a longtime disciple of Pūjya Gurudev, was entrusted with the work. He completed the first ten chapters, and, in order to hasten the work, Gurudev instructed another veteran, Śrī T. Seshadri of Madurai, to complete the rest. At the same time, Gurudev offered the entire amount of Guru-dakṣiṇā that came in after the jñāna yajña in Chennai in February 1984 to facilitate the publication work. Śrī Kesava Reddy also offered a substantial amount to take the work forward.

Smt. Leela Nambiar, Smt. Padma Narasimhan, and Śrī Deepak Shah were among those who supported the translation of *The Holy Geeta* commentary in Tamil, which appeared initially in two volumes. Later, it was split into slim volumes with individual chapters, making it handy for the devotees to carry to the

yajñaśālā. Swami Vedatmananda and Swamini Sumedhananda offered their scholarly help in translating a variety of books into Tamil.

Swami Sridharananda, who is based in Tiruchi, took charge of Tamil Publications in 2002 and has been doing excellent work, supervising and standardizing the translations. Gearing toward the Chinmaya Birth Centenary Celebrations, work is underway to translate and publish the entire set of Upaniṣad commentaries by Gurudev in Tamil.

Kannada

Publications in Kannada flourished under the inspiring guidance of Swami Brahmananda, who personally translated many of Gurudev's books and also wrote a number of new books and commentaries. Under his leadership, the Ācāryas of the Karnataka region contributed actively. *Guru Tattva* and *Sādhanā Saurabha* are compilations of articles written by the Ācāryas of Karnataka. Swami Adityananda has translated *Manaḥ Śodhanam* and *Purajana Gītā*.

Śrī C. L. Purushothama Rao and Śrī B. S. Vishwanath Rao, ardent devotees of Pūjya Gurudev, rendered invaluable service by translating many of the commentaries by Gurudev on the Upaniṣads, *Vivekacūḍāmaṇi*, and other texts. Perhaps the first book to be translated into Kannada was Gurudev's commentary on *Bhaja Govindam*, translated by Śrī B. K. Thimmappa. Some of the other translators before the turn of the century were Śrī A. S. Venugopal Rao, Śrī B. S. Satyanarayana, and Śrī Suresh Kumar. In the recent years, Smt. Uma Srikanta, Śrī Basavalingappa, Śrī Madhusudan, and others have come forward to continue the translations of popular titles.

Special mention needs to be made of the beautiful souvenirs in English brought out by the Karnataka region. Many of these are collector's items. The latest one, titled *Chinmaya Vaibhavam*, published in January 2013, is a coffee table edition, replete with vivid and vibrant pictures that bring alive Pūjya Gurudev and his times.

Bengali

Pūjya Gurudev's keen power of observation and deep sense of intuition helped him to identify a person of worth. One such person was Śrī Kamal Kumar Ghosh, who used to compose poems in Bengali at leisure. Once he composed the entire *Gītā* in Bengali verse. He sought permission from Pūjya Gurudev to translate his books into Bengali. Though Gurudev had never met him, he not only granted him permission, but sent him wholehearted blessings in an inspiring letter. In the course of time, Kamal Kumar Ghosh became the mainstay for the publication of Bengali literature in Chinmaya Mission.

Other Indian Languages

Chinmaya Mission books have been translated into other Indian languages like Oriya, Assamese, Sindhi, and Urdu. The work continues and new translations are going to the press even as this book is being written.

Translations in European and Other Languages

Globally, books have been translated into languages like French and German. In 2013, Martin Vinkler's translation of *Tattva Bodha* in the Czech language was released. Swami Swaroopananda's *Ik Oṅkār* has been translated into Spanish. The latest to come out is the *A Manual of Self-Unfoldment*, translated by Daniela Badea into the Romanian language.

Romanian translation of A Manual of Self-Unfoldment ▼

◄ *Tattva Bodha in Korean language*

Tattva Bodha translated into Czech in 2013 ▶

German

Ursula Zieschang, also known as Urmila, translated the commentaries on *Īśāvāsya Upaniṣad* and *Ātma Bodha* into German. *Īśāvāsya Upaniṣad* was published by Chinmaya Publication Trust, Madras, in 1972. The German translation of *Bhaja Govindam* by Urmila was circulated during March 8–12, 1971, when Gurudev gave classes at the Bircher-Benner Klinik. There is also an extant manuscript of her German translation of *Kenopaniṣad*.

▲ *Īśāvāsya Upaniṣad in German*

French

Swamini Umananda, known earlier as Brni. Bhakti Chaitanya, has contributed a lot to the Chinmaya Mission activities in France. She has

translated *The Holy Geeta* into the French language, which has already come out in the third edition. Other books that have been translated and published in French are *Meditation and Life, Self-Unfoldment, Ageless Guru*, Gurudev's commentary on *Sādhana Pañcakam*, Swami Tejomayananda's commentaries on *Upadeśa Sāra* and *Tattva Bodha*, and his composition *Dhyāna Svarūpam* with explanations.

Souvenirs

The practice of distributing *Yagna Prasad* booklets after each yajña gave way to the publication of souvenirs in the 1960s. Though the immediate purpose of these souvenirs was to raise funds for the yajña through advertisements, each one of them carried precious collections of articles and other material. Many of them were so good that they were later reprinted as full-fledged books.

Special mention must be made of *Hail Renaissance*, the souvenir that was brought out to commemorate the Silver Jubilee Yajña in Hyderabad (December 16, 1956 to January 5, 1957) and the second volume of *Hail Renaissance* that was brought out on the occasion of the Golden Jubilee Yajña (January 26 to February 15, 1959) in Bangalore. These two volumes are of historical

ANNOUNCING—

Hail Renaissance

VOLUME II

BOARD OF EDITORS

Miss Sulochana Menon	...	...	Kerala
Miss Laxmi Reddy	...	...	Hyderabad
Mrs. Sheila Puri	...	...	New Delhi
Mrs. Manorama Aggrawal	...	...	Allahabad
Mrs. Sheila Dewan	...	...	Bombay
Mrs. Sundaram	...	...	Madras
Mrs. Kamala Reddy	...	...	Bangalore
Mrs. Lakshmikantam	...	...	Madurai
Mrs. Radha Namboripad	...	...	Tinnevelli

Miss SULOCHANA MENON
Publication in-charge,

" Dwaraka "
Sasthamangalam
TRIVANDRUM
30th September 1958

On the occasion of the 50th Yagna to be held from 26th Jan. to 15th Feb. 1959 in Bangalore, we wish to bring out another Souvenir "Hail Renaissance" Volume II, like the one we had already published during the Silver Jubilee Yagna in Hyderabad.

Hope your good self is well aware of the Yagna activities of Sri Swamiji, and you have also attended the Yagna Session yourself when held in your own city. Probably you too had contributed to the first Volume. Once again your good self is requested to co-operate with us and help us in our noble endeavour, by contributing articles to the same.

Sri Swamiji is very particular that the articles should not be a glorification of the Swami but it must be a report of your own personal reactions to the Yagna, indicating the possible results it can have in the

44

Renaissance of Hinduism.   The following suggestions will give you an idea as to what fields can be covered by your articles.

SUGGESTIONS :—

  I. *Your own personal reaction :*— a) The Discourses–its Neo-Hindu ideas. b) The discipline of the Yagna Sala. c) The rituals— Haven and Akhanda Kirtan and their interpretations. d) The picnic and its Sanyas spirit. e) The meditation classes, Japa practices, text books taken in the morning classes etc.

 II. *Social reactions of the Yagna :*— a) Communal brotherhood: b) Sense of unity; c) Spirit of Nationalism: d) New interpretations of the methods, goal and the way of life.

III. *Reactions in homes :*— a) New spirit of mutul reverence. b) Spirit of understanding and co-operation among the members of family; c) Reaction on children.

 IV. *Mission and its activities :*— a) The weekly sat-sang. b) Monthly meetings :   c) The Conference.

  V. Publication in general :— a) Books and Magazines; b) Free book distribution.

 VI. *Correspondence :*— Comfort, consolations, solution of problems, liquidation of doubts, encouragement, sympathies received through letters.

VII. *Improvements* you would suggest on the Yagnasala, publications, Mission and its activities etc.

VIII. *Bhikshas* and *padapujas.*

 IX. *Swamiji as our guest —* by the hosts who had the chance to enter- tain Swamiji for a number of days under their roof.

The articles should not exceed more then 2,000 words and it must reach the above address by the 1st of December. You may send us photographs if any. We hope to publish it in Jan. 1959, during the 50th Yagna–Session proposed now to be held in Bangalore. Hope to hear from you soon.

Thanking you and eagerly looking forward to receive your write-up.

Thy own Sevika,
SULOCHANA MENON,
Publication-in-charge (Souvenir)

importance and carry many articles by devotees on how the jñāna yajñas had transformed them in myriad unimaginable ways.

The popular book *Sankara the Missionary* was brought out as a yajña souvenir in 1978 by Śrī M. Vasudevan Nair on behalf of Chinmaya Mission Jamshedpur. Gurudev used to conduct quarterly yajñas in Jamshedpur. The set of three souvenirs *Glory of Krishna, Glory of Ganesha,* and *Glory of the Mother* were thus published in 1982, 1986, and 1990 respectively. Gurudev took a personal interest in the compilation of these books and corresponded with Śrī Vasudevan Nair regularly. The illustrations of various forms of Gaṇeśa were sourced by Swami Brahmananda and sent to him. *Glory of the Mother* was written by Gurudev during his early years in Uttarkashi, an inspired outpouring sent to Śrī Bhaskara Menon, and Śrī Vasudevan used the handwritten manuscript to bring out the souvenir.

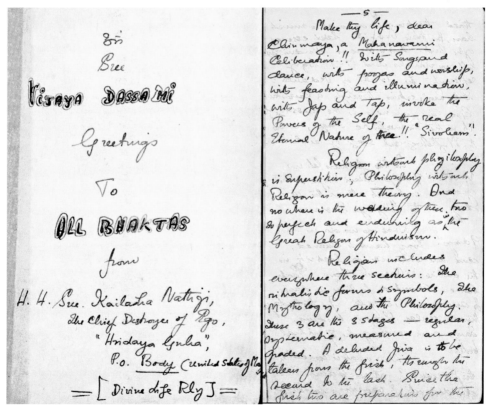

▲ *Sample pages of the manuscript in Gurudev's own handwriting. This was the source of the book* Glory of the Mother.

Gurudev maintained a diary written in pencil during his travels in the Himalayan region in 1948, before he received sannyāsa dīkṣā and settled down to study with Swami Tapovan Maharaj. It was published in the *National Herald* as a series of eight articles from May 1948 onward. Later, this diary was handed over to Bharati Sukhatankar, who brought it out as a souvenir for Gurudev's 328th Jñāna Yajña in Delhi in March 1982. Gurudev's sketches that enlivened the travelogue in the diary were also reproduced in the souvenir. This is the book we know today as *My Trek through Uttarkhand*.

▲ Pencil ▶ sketches made by Pūjya Gurudev during his trek through Uttarkhand

Hanumat Vibhūti was another souvenir compiled and designed by Bharati Sukhatankar on the occasion of the first Mastakābhiṣekam of Hanumān in Sidhbari on October 10, 1982. She has an interesting story to narrate about it:

> We had started our search for a professional calligrapher to do the title lettering for the cover. Also, Br. Vivek Chaitanya (now Swami Tejomayananda) had sent eight selected verses from the *Rāmacaritmānas*[7] to be included in the souvenir. These verses, too, needed to be calligraphed carefully. But where was the calligrapher? Where were we going to find him?
>
> And then I received a message from Swamiji: "I will be in Delhi on Sunday morning. Hope to see you with the cover completed and other illustrations for *Hanumat Vibhūti*." This was Saturday evening. I went into a double spin and tottered at the door of Madhav Naik, my neighbor, who did the illustrations for the book. "The time is too short," he said. "Who will do it for us, that, too, by tomorrow morning?" My head spun and went on the blink. Who indeed? With hunched shoulders and clouded brow and ten kilos of lead in my heart, I came back home. Glum. Dismal. Dejected.
>
> It happens. We work toward a goal, but something at the last moment prevents us from achieving it. Here, we were running out of time. "This was perhaps the only chance we had to show Swamiji the final look of the souvenir. And we couldn't," was another profoundly deep, dark thought I had. We couldn't find one single calligrapher in the huge sprawling capital of India!
>
> Just then the doorbell rang. There was Madhav, and behind him, a shy, nondescript, unshaven young man. Madhav

---

[7] These verses are inscribed on marble in the pedestal of Śrī Hanumān's statue in Sidhbari.

introduced him as an etching artist from Jaipur who had, minutes back, come to him looking for work. "I engrave on metal," said the young man and told us that his name was Ram Sevak. "Naik sahib told me that you need some lettering work done. I can do English as well as Devanāgarī calligraphy."

My eyes grew wide as saucers. I gushed him in. "Come, come. Where would you like to sit? Where would you like to work? Will you be comfortable at the dining table? What will you need? Paper? Poster paints? Ink? Pens? Brushes?"

"No, thank you." Ram Sevak had his own paper, pens, brushes, and etching inks, which he proceeded to take out of his briefcase. He just wanted a table and good light. Those were easily provided.

Now came the tricky part — selecting the style and size of the lettering. After some back-and-forth discussions, we arrived at a consensus. Endless cups of coffee and a staggering tower of sandwiches saw us through to midnight and after. Finally, there were five covers for Swamiji to choose from, a stylishly written flyleaf page and the *Rāmacaritmānas* verses in a neat Devanāgarī script. Ram Sevak stood up, yawned, and stretched. We all yawned and stretched. Whoosh! It was done! Finally, finally, finally!

प्रनवउँ पवनकुमार खल बन पावक ग्यान घन।
जासु हृदय आगार बसहिं राम सर-चाप धर॥

राम नाम मनिदीप धरु जीह देहरीं द्वार।
तुलसी भीतर बाहरेहुँ जौं चाहिस उजियार॥

▲ *Verses from Rāmacaritmānas in calligraphy*

"What should we pay you?" we asked him. "Pay me? Nothing. Nothing at all. No, don't try to force anything on me. I won't take it. Besides, I am a bhakta. This was worship for me. Hanumān's work is my work. It is late. I will go now. My relatives in Daryaganj will be waiting for me." And Ram Sevak disappeared like a twinkling star into the cool dark September night.

The following morning, we were bright and early at the Nambiars' doorstep. How can I describe what it felt to meet Swamiji each time? The anticipation was always palpable. But today, there was a silly light-heartedness, which had everything to do with our God-sent calligrapher from Jaipur.

Swamiji finished breakfast, came to the living room, settled himself into a large sofa, while we clustered on the carpet at his feet. "Let me see," he said, and put out his hand for the Hanumat Vibhūti portfolio. He looked carefully at all the pages and asked a few questions. "Ads plenty?" "Good quotation from the printer?" His eyebrows shot up appreciatively when he came to the cover and the calligraphed verses from *Rāmacaritmānas*. Behind two of the covers he wrote, "My I choice," and "My II choice."

Then we told him the story of Ram Sevak, how he came and worked through half the night, and how he refused payment for his work. Swamiji listened intently to our story, then said, "Don't forget to send him a copy of the souvenir when it is out."

We looked at each other. In our excitement, none of us had bothered to ask for his address, either in Delhi or in Jaipur. Swamiji removed his glasses, looked at the ceiling, and closed his eyes. "So," he said, stroking his beard. "You don't know who came and did the calligraphy for you! Splendid! You don't have his address! Excellent! You don't know where to locate him! Tremendous!"

Then, after a small pause, he added: "Make no mistake, it was Hanumān himself. That is how he works." Swamiji smiled softly.

We found our hair standing on end. We, students of Vedānta, who always sought to rationalize, couldn't comprehend divine Grace when we came face to face with it, for it couldn't be refracted through our intellectual prism. Tat-padaṁ darśitam yena, tasmai śrī gurave namaḥ: Prostrations unto the Guru who showed the Supreme. At his feet, we felt gently chastised and humbled.

▲ *Original cover of the* Hanumat Vibhūti *souvenir*

Prasāda Pustikās

The *Yagna Prasad* of the olden days has taken a new avatar with the slim 'prasāda pustikās' which are distributed to everyone at the end of a jñāna yajña. People take away these thought-provoking, tiny booklets, which can be put easily into a handbag or large pocket and read at leisure anywhere. They have become popular as return gifts at family gatherings, religious functions, and occasions like birthdays and weddings as well.

Prasāda is meant for all and children clamor for their share! So Chinmaya Gardens in Coimbatore has brought out a prasāda pustikā for them, titled *Inspiring Children from Ancient India*.

Books for Children

Pūjya Gurudev enchanted children and mesmerized them with his extraordinary talent for storytelling. He entered their world and became one with them in spirit; he could communicate at their wavelength to pass on the values and traditions of Indian culture.

In 1968, he published the first of the three volumes of *Tell Me a Story*, to be distributed as yajña prasāda. These stories were mostly adaptations from the Purāṇas and other popular traditional lore. They were written by Brni. Sarada (later known as Swamini Saradapriyananda), Bharati Sukhatankar, and Swamiji himself, though he preferred to remain incognito. Two or three stories were also written by Urmila. At the end of each story, the writer's name was mentioned.

◀ *Letter dated June 14, 1968 to Bharati Naik (now Bharati Sukhatankar)*

I had been waiting for it all these years.

I had asked, begged, requested, ordered, commanded, paid, never I got anything satisfactory so far.

I used some of them — so so. I even brought out a small book Dharma Kahāniyāṁ. They were flat.

I want round, healthy, robust, talking, speaking, lively, stories, dashing in action — suggestive for the innocent minds of the children.

Let us complete Ramayan please. Destroy Ravana and return to Ayodhya.

▲ *Gurudev's letter dated July 5, 1968 to Bharati Naik*

ℰℰ *Now look — a mother loves even a Caesarian child — even if it has polio, even if it is ugly or very underdeveloped. And in fact, no one is utterly useless in life. Therefore your stories are to be used and respected.*

When I said they must have a little more stuff, I meant they must be fed a little more carefully so that they should present a pulpy look with rounded limbs and giggling mouth. We can fatten a story by nature, character, speech or emotion.

Nature — must be only suggestive with fine inconspicuous strokes slender.

Character — must waft their distinct flavour clearly, not through words directly, but by actions or through words of others in the story.

Speech — in some stories, the conversation is their very heart.

Emotion — the reader should be made to walk through vestibule of different emotions.

The rest of the ideas regarding stories had been sent to you in our leaflet: "Tell, never preach a story." This I had sent you a couple of months back from here.

It is usual in Hinduism that when parents go to religious festivals or ritualistic yajñas, they bring home something to be shared by all, and this is called prasāda. Till now, in our yajñas, we had been distributing prasāda only for the parents, as my children were then too small to take in any prasāda. Now the Bala Vihar children have started not only demanding, but even invading my yajñasālās...

Therefore, it was conceived that we must have some prasāda which parents can share with their children. And thus, I have, at this time, compiled some stories 'retold.' They are not original ones — they are all adaptations made by two brahmacāriṇis, Sarada and Bharathi, and two stories are done by a Swami who chooses to remain incognito. Almost all the stories have depths, especially the stories adapted by the Swami. Parents can discuss those significances ....

I have strewn kīrtan-bits all over. During the reading, or telling of the stories, at these appropriate places, the children listening and the reader must together sing loudly the kīrtan-line. In this way, the dhun[8] and the story become associated with each other in the mind of the student ....

---

[8] Musical chanting

> I am also planning a *Rāmāyaṇa* for children, amply illustrated. Get the volume for your children. Each day read out to them only one chapter or section. The following day, if they are able to repeat all the stories so far read, with names of persons and places, then only proceed further ....
>
> Please help us to help your children, the future of the nation itself.
>
> – Swami Chinmayananda
> From the preface to *Tell Me a Story*

The next major children's book was *Bāla Rāmāyaṇam*, released by Swamiji in October 1968. This book, and the next one, *Bāla Bhāgavatam*, which was released in early 1969, were authored by 'Chinmaya and Bharathi.' The books were actually written by Bharati Sukhatankar, but Swamiji sowed the seed, explained the whole idea, gave detailed instructions to her, and monitored the work closely, giving suggestions, advice, and admonitions time to time:

▲ *Excerpt from Gurudev's letter to Bharati dated May 18, 1968*

The national history, geography, philosophy, social customs, plants, birds, mountains, rivers, sacred places, character, ideals, all can be woven into them [the stories] and held up for our children. Make them weep — pant — surge — ready for action — ready for sacrifice. Puranas are a treasure trove.

As the story progressed and the installments were sent to Swamiji, he guided her step by step:

In a hurry-burry, don't kill Rāvaṇa. Number One: a criminal like him must die slowly. Sudden death is a blessing. Number Two: Rāvaṇa was a tapasvin. He had acquired many blessings from the Lord, and therefore, in your hurry-burry, if you kill him only half, he will get up with a vengeance in your bosom again with all the ten heads efficiently working to destroy all the good in the bosom. In that section, please go a little slow, painting thick the incorrigible devil in Rāvaṇa — uncompromising, unrepentant, with inhuman audacity and vicious purposefulness. When the disease is serious, acute, treatment is to be very thorough. Slowly paint how, in the ignominy of his death, vanity in him gets slowly dripped out, until at last he realizes his folly. Show the sense of justice in Rāma in honoring and respecting his great enemy.

Through the story, he was not only reaching out to the children, but teaching Bharati as well:

In life, you can't escape criticism. And yet, Valmiki is trying to give us a set of ideal pictures in Rāma's life. The ideal son of Dasaratha, yet caused his death; an ideal brother, yet refused to oblige Bharath; an ideal husband in the jungle, but caused Sītā to prove her purity, because she is no more a mere wife of Rāma, but she is also the consort of the King and therefore the Queen of the people. Caesar's wife must be above suspicion ....

As an ideal Swami, if I retire to Uttarkashi, the Mission workers will murmur and grumble. If in the service of the people you dash about in the country and kick and fret and fume for the sake of efficiency, you are an unspiritual Swami. Wear decent clothes — it is too luxurious; wear merely one piece of cloth — he is showing off; wear only a langoti — he is indecent. Nobody in the world can satisfy everybody — not even the Gods!

Swamiji conferred praise at the right time and encouraged her to continue with increased enthusiasm and vigor.

The work is brilliant, and I can see Hanuman now permanently established on the very table at which you work. This has become really a glorious sadhana for you and a splendid seva yagna for the children.

Now you must have realised that you are a born writer of childrens' literature. Very few can do it. It is a God-given blessing. Cultivate it. Develop it. India needs it. World is waiting for it.

Throw a little more colour into the emotions. The children leaving Dasaratha is a scene where our children must shed tears!! Sitha leaving Janaka is another instance. Bring out all emotions vividly. Let them weep in sympathy, love, affection, tenderness, devotion, obedience, sigh in relief, heave in the heroism felt, courtesy shown, goodness manifest.

It is in these deep reactions that children get these qualities ever fixed upon their heart.

Let them not ever forget that this was India — our Bharat. Rama-Lakshman-Bharat represent the ideal Hindu — the perfect Aryan — the exemplary Indian Janata. Guha and others represent the perfect people. Paint it thicker ..... take them all along the path of emotional ups and downs, through ashramas, river beds, mountains — pause them to watch flowers, trees, tendrils — animals, insects — point out to them moon, sunrise, stars, sky, clouds.

Let us read about the writing of *Bāla Rāmāyaṇa* in Bharati's own words:

> I wrote the *Bāla Rāmāyaṇa* in 1968. That was the time when Swamiji was in Uttarkashi, teaching *Vivekacūḍāmaṇi* to the first batch of brahmacārīs. Urmila (Ursula Zieschang), a German lady and the only foreigner there, stayed in Uttarkashi for the full three months, helping Swamiji with the correspondence.
>
> I used to write 20–25 pages and send them to him. He would send the pages back to me with corrections. I didn't know how to type. I wrote to him with apologies for inflicting my handwriting on him and mentioned that I was making an attempt to learn typing. He wrote back, "Don't waste your time. Your handwriting

is quite easy on the eyes. I can read it very well. The Lord has put in this world people to do the donkey's work for creative people like you and me. Take the manuscript to our Urmila. She will type and prepare it for the press." He had dictated this letter to Urmila! At that time she did not know me, nor had I met her.

The letter was duly sent to me. When Urmila returned to Delhi, I went to her house to meet her. I rode a bicycle and had my hair in two pigtails like any traditional Indian girl of those days. I took the manuscript, some paper, typing ribbons, and so on, to avoid expenses for her. I did not know she was working as the administrative officer for the World Bank in Delhi! When I entered, she was sitting there, polishing her nails nonchalantly. "Just leave it there," she said casually. Seeing me taken aback, she continued, "I will see to it later. I am sorry. I have an appointment with my hairdresser." I gave her my telephone number in case she needed any clarification and then cycled back home.

▲ Urmila is standing in the row behind Gurudev, at the extreme left, and next to her is Bharati. Shiela Puri is seated fourth from right and Sheela Sharma is seated on the extreme left.

Later on, when we had become good friends, Urmila told me that she had intended to let me know where I got off! We had a good laugh over it. We had met Swamiji around the same time, and we became soulmates in the later years. I am yet to come across anyone who was so tuned to his way of thinking. Though a German, with no knowledge of Sanskrit, and hardly any knowledge of Hindi, she responded instinctively and intuitively to the essence of Vedānta.

While writing the story, Bharati had also done some line drawings and sent them to Swamiji along with the manuscript. Swamiji included these as illustrations in the book. He also gave her specific instructions about the cover. The sketch of Śrī Rāma handing over the pādukās to Bharata and blessing him was chosen for the front cover, and he told her to write "Ram Ram" in Devanāgarī all around the sketch.

Gurudev's message on the ▶
flyleaf of Bharati's copy of
Bala Ramayanam

May you bring out many more
such books to serve the children.

Swamiji gave instructions not only about the writing, but all aspects of the book. He told her how to ink the sketches and how to pack and send the manuscripts. He explained the proofing symbols and how to maintain a record of the manuscript pages dispatched and the corrected ones received. He discussed the size of the pages, the quality of paper, the binding, the dust cover, the number of copies to be printed, and he calculated the sale price per copy.

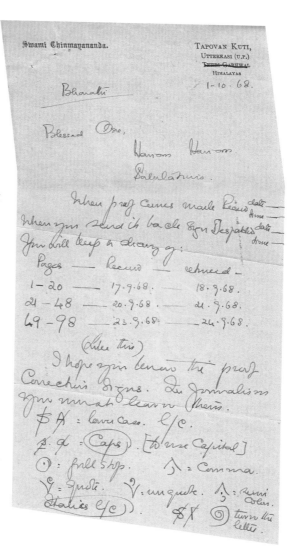

When proof comes, mark received date — time —

When you send it back sign despatched date — time —

You will keep a diary of

Pages — Received — Returned

1–20   — 17.9.68 —   18.9.68

21–48 — 20.9.68 —   21.9.68

49–98 — 23.9.68 —   24.9.68

(Like this)

I hope you know the proof correction signs. In journalism, you must learn them.

Your letter (4th July) and the "Sitha Search" portion. In each portion, your devotion for Rama clearly distills out to the surface. May that Ayodhya Pathi's grace add efficiency to your pen.

The sketches on thicker paper — polished one side — is better for blocks. But ordinary paper also is sufficient. But they may shrink under ink — India ink. Sanfroid paper is not available.

These card-papers come in big sheets. Get it cut in Time magazine size. If you have already finished some sketches, they need not be redone please.

Love to your mother. May the Grace of Bhageerathi help her to come out of her illness quickly.

◄ *A page from Gurudev's letter to Bharati, dated August 6, 1968*

As it is, estimates are coming:

5000 copies 200 pages Ballarpur 36 the offset paper, open binding Time size — soft board cover — with dust cover — 1/4 cloth bound — 20 sketches etc. comes to Rs. 4.65 per book. We must pull it down to 3–4 so that we may be able to sell at 8 or 10. We will have to give 35% for book stalls, agents etc. — their transport etc. — and about 25,000 investment interest!!

Ganga Mai ki Jai. What have you done — for you I have now become a baniya in Himalayas!! But it is for Ram and so no fault in it.

[handwritten note:] I am searching for verses for the sketches. In some of the sketches we could use a bit of the thick charcoal pencil! To make strokes broad & bold.

◀ From a letter
to Bharati dated
August 9, 1968

I am searching for verses for the sketches. In some of the sketches we could use a bit of the thick charcoal pencil to make strokes broad and bold.

▲ *Original cover of*
Bāla Bhāgavatam

After the completion of *Bāla Rāmāyaṇa*, Swamiji kept up the momentum and asked Bharati to write *Bāla Bhāgavatam*. He sent a bunch of *Bhāgavatam* books to her in September 1968. She took them to Simla, where the work began and was completed within a few months.

Sketches and ślokas ▶
on page 1 of
Bāla Bhāgavatam

After almost a decade, in 1979–80, the *Tarangini* series of eleven books were published one by one. These stories were written mostly by Swamini Saradapriyananda and edited by Bharati. They became a part of the curriculum in Chinmaya Vidyalayas as an aid to the moral education classes. After another decade or so, these were replaced in the school curriculum by the *Garden of Life* series written by Radhika Krishnakumar and published by Macmillan. Since these were more interactive and colorful, they carried a greater appeal for the children.

The beginning of the twenty-first century saw a resurgence and blossoming of children's books in Chinmaya Mission. The *Balvihar* magazine brought out compilations of materials published in the magazine — *The Balvihar Book of Picture Parables*, *The Balvihar Book of Gurudev's Tales*, *The Balvihar Book of Train the Brain*, *The Balvihar Book of Jokes*, and so on. A revised version of the *Tell Me a Story* series, with attractive illustrations on glossy art paper, was produced by Parveen Bahl. She also brought out more colorful versions of the *Tarangini* series of books.

Brni. Nishita Chaitanya's (now Swamini Supriyananda) creative writing and fabulous illustrations bring alive Kṛṣṇa, Gaṇeśa, and Śiva through imaginative adaptations to suit the modern lifestyle of small children. *Ganesha Goes to a Party, Krishna Photocopies Himself, Krishna Rocks, Krishna's Butter Bash, Krishna: An Invisible Friend, Shiva's Fish Swish*, and other such titles have proved to be hot favorites with children. The more recent series on Hanumān — *Go Hanuman! Go!* and *Hanuman's Big Gig* — have also captured the imagination of children by presenting the stories in a way that they can relate to.

Please refer to the chapter 'The Literary Trail' in the book *Our Children, Our Future* (The *Mananam* Series) for additional details about children's literature in Chinmaya Mission, and the website *www. chinmayakids.org* for children.

Publications by Various Wings of the Mission

The various wings of Chinmaya Mission, like the Bala Vihar, Chinmaya Yuva Kendra and Vanaprastha Sansthan periodically publish literature relevant to their activities and areas of interest. For instance, the Bala Vihar in Chennai produces its own book annually, based on the theme of the year. In Houston, Acharya Darshana Nanavaty has written a series of graded books for Bala Vihar, creatively crafted to suit the different age groups.

The Vanaprastha Sansthan has fielded many books which are well researched and offer practical guidance to senior citizens about how to handle various aspects of life in the sunset years. *Jarāvasthā Kaise Jiye* (*How to Live in Old Age*) by Swami Shankarananda, *Growing Divine* by Swami Yogasthananda, *Jarā Svāsthya Vijñān* (*Science of Old Age Health*) by Dr. Sajjan Singh are some of these.

The Chinmaya Yuva Kendra has been prolific in the output of books related to the major projects that they have taken up in the last few years. *Gita for Yuva, Bhaja Govindam for Yuva, Illustrations of the Illustrator, The Other Way, Drop, Transforming Lives, Rama: the Man of Treta Yuga,* and *Ganga: More Than a River,* are some of these. *Seeking,* which can also be read as *Sea King,* is a very interesting book written by Swami Mitrananda about his annual quiet time at sea, completely cut off from the rest of the world.

Chinmaya International Foundation has its own research publications, which are unique and off beat. While some of them are scholarly expositions, others are treasures to be cherished by lay people as well. Noteworthy among these are the *Sukti Sudha* and the *Holy Gita Ready Reference*. The chapter on publications 'From Thought to Word' in the book *Unto Research* in the Mananam Series throws light on some of the books published by the Foundation.

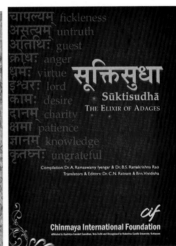

Audio Recordings

Right from the beginning, Swamiji's talks had been recorded off and on by many people. By the sixties, Swamiji started making full use of the radio as a means of mass communication. He gave three talks on 'The Age of the Spiritual Quest,' which were broadcast on the All India Radio and later published as articles in three issues of *Tyagi* from July 1961 onward. His talk on 'Sankara: The Mighty Missionary' was aired on the All India Radio (AIR) in 1963. Three talks on 'Bhaja Govindam Plan' (AIR, Madras, 1963) and 'Peace through Religion' (AIR, Coimbatore, 1968) were among many other such talks. A set of six introductory talks on the *Bhagavad-gītā* was aired by the All India Radio, Delhi, and many other AIR stations in 1970.

<table>
<tr><td>

SWAMIJI'S RADIO TALK
on
" SHANKARA—THE MIGHTY MISSIONARY '

Listen to Madras A.I.R. at 8.45 P.M. on April 20, 1963.

We have been receiving complaints that there was no reception at all at certain places like Allahabad, Bombay etc., of the previous broadcasts. We request them all to write to their nearest A.I.R. broadcasting station to re-broadcast the same talks, under arrangement with A.I.R., Madras. This problem will be solved if the A.I.R. broadcasts Swamiji's talks in such wavelengths as would reach the entire country.

(E.D.)

</td><td>

A.I.R. BROADCAST

We understand that the A. I. R. Delhi has directed all Station Directors to broadcast Swamiji's six talks which constitute an introduction to Bhagavad Geeta. Each Station would be putting them out according to their convenience. Delhi Station has planned to broadcast them in March.

All are requested to contact the Station Directors of their individual locality, and ascertain the date of the broadcast. You will carefully listen to them.

If we find that these talks have been effective we shall then try to take up a series of daily talks on the entire Bhagavad Geeta. In these talks the thesis is that the Geeta is a Scripture of the teen-agers, our disillusioned and confused growing generation.

—EDITOR

</td></tr>
</table>

▲ *Published in* Tapovan Prasad, *March 1963*

▲ *Published in* Tapovan Prasad, *May 1970*

Some talks were broadcast from other countries as well. The United Hindu Organization arranged to broadcast Swamiji's talk over Trinidad Radio on the occasion of Trinidad Independence Day on August 31, 1967. In the same year, Swamiji delivered a series of talks over GIT Radio, Demerara, Guyana, under the title 'Teachings from the Pages of Scriptures.'

One of the early audio recordings done professionally at HMV (His Master's Voice) studios was the talk on *Bhaja Govindam*. In 1967, Swamiji recorded three talks — 'Act Now,' 'Faith that Revives,' and 'Laugh Away' — on extended play discs (EP). The recording was done in P. M. T. Studios, Kuala Lumpur, Malaysia.

The *Art of Man-making* was a series of talks on the *Gītā* presented by All India Radio, Hyderabad, from November 18 to December 2, 1970. Someone in the government echelons of power felt the talks were not secular, and, hence, they were discontinued when Swamiji completed Chapter 10. These talks became very popular in book form and are ordered in bulk by educational institutions and management schools even today. A sequel has been brought out since then to cover the rest of the chapters by compiling portions from Gurudev's other talks.

Pūjya Gurudev relaxes with ▶ a cup of coffee in between the recording sessions at the All India Radio, Hyderabad.

◀ Lakshmi Reddy records the chanting to accompany Pūjya Gurudev at the All India Radio station in Hyderabad in the seventies.

Swami Chinmayananda
Chinmaya Books (U.S.A.)
P.O. Box 2753
Napa, California 94558

St. John's
Newfoundland
Canada
June 3, 1975

Blessed One,

    Hari om!   *Hari om!*   *Salutations!*

Time flies: last I wrote to you a full month ago on May 3, 1975. During the last one month, we had served again three centres, each with a session of ten days: at the Confederation College, Thunder Bay, Ontario; at Cleveland State University, Ohio; and at the Memorial University of Newfoundland, St. John's, Newfoundland. In all these places the enthusiasm was good, and the impression left appears to be deep and enduring.

The Chinmaya Publications (West) in Napa, California, have decided to build up a tape-library and have requested all centres to provide them with a copy of the tape-recordings of our talks, as a contribution from each centre. The tape-library will prepare copies from our master-copy and distribute them to those who request for these talks.

I had, in India, prepared some hundred and odd short talks (each 10 to 15 minutes) developing the Geeta ideas to serve the teenagers and creative men who aspire to unfold their own faculties, who desire to end their hang-ups, and who want to bring a larger efficiency into their fields of work. These talks are being professionally now made on fourteen cassettes and the album, The Art of Man-making, will be ready in a month's time, available at our Napa office ($50.00). These talks were very popular in India where they were broadcast on the All-India Radio.

We did hint in our previous report that for all these activities we will be needing funds. This initial fund is now to be raised by accepting 200 "Contributing Members" screened and recommended by the Directors and finally accepted by Swamiji and "confirmed" by the C.M. (W). Each of such confirmed "Contributing Members" will pay $10 a month for two years. We will not accept more than 200 members at anytime. Other willing contributors will be held on our waiting list; whenever a "Contributing Member" defaults, then a member from the waiting list will be taken up, screened, voted and confirmed by Sri Swamiji. All "Contributing Members" will receive (unless they default) all issues of <u>Mananam</u> and some of the books we publish during each year. I am sure you will pass on this "scheme" only to persons whom you recommend us to accept as members. Let them send their first contribution through you so that we know who recommended whom, among our 200 members. The "Contributing Members" can pay in lump $120 for the year or $240 for both the years.

The set of 14 Cassette in which Swami Chinmayananda has given 114 short talks on the ART OF MAN-MAKING based on Geeta ideas is now ready for dispatch at NAPA, the C.P. (W) Headquarters. Some 142 sets have already been sold out and we are now ordering more sets to be dispatched out of U.S.A. Centres. There is a growing demand for them. I am told that $50 per set is the cheapest price in the market for such an elaborate educational 14-Cassette Set. Every Indian family in America and Canada can afford it and they must have them for themselves and for their growing children.

I am extremely thankful to the thousands who gave me their best attention and sincere participation during the sessions, and the hundreds of volunteers who helped to organize all these 20 sessions.

Upon the team of inspired men and women who so joyously served in the Camp at Humbolt, I invoke the Lord's Grace and Blessings.

With Love and Om,
Thy Own Self,
Chinmayananda

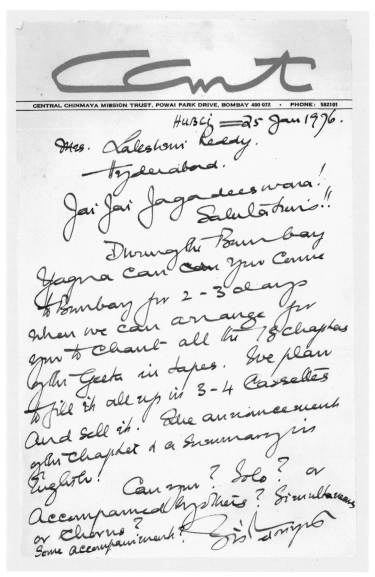

During the Bombay yagna, can you come to Bombay for 2–3 days when we can arrange for you to chant all the 18 chapters of the Geeta on tapes. We plan to fill it all up in 3–4 cassettes and sell it. The announcement of the chapter and a summary in English!

Can you? Solo? Or accompanied by others? Simultaneous or chorus? Some accompaniment?

The audio recordings of Vedic chants, stotras, and bhajans by Swami Brahmananda have been a source of delight to devotees. His deep and resonant voice, clear pronunciation, and intensity of spiritual fervor lift the listener to a meditative state with spontaneous ease. The entire *Bhagavad-gītā* chanted in his rich voice is a treasure cherished by many devotees and used as a guide for *Gītā* chanting classes. *Prabhat Sudha* and *Stotra Mala* are eternal favorites. *Śrī Vishnu Sahasranama, Śrī Lalita Sahasranama,* and *Śrī Shivasahasranama* create a divine atmosphere and help the seekers to chant along effortlessly. *Tapovananjali* and *Tattvamala* invoke the blessings of the Gurus. The *Navagraha Sookta* and even the simple chant of Oṁ Namo Nārāyanāya create a divine ambience wherever they are played.

The *Gītā* chanting competitions for children all over India necessitated a standardized learning tool. Every year, a different chapter of the *Gītā* is taken up, and the corresponding 'Gītā Learning Aid Kits' are produced in Coimbatore. Half a line of each śloka is chanted in Swami Brahmananda's rich voice in a 'lead-and-follow' format, making learning easy.

Today, the audio cassettes of yesteryears have yielded place to CDs and DVDs. The discourses of Pūjya Gurudev and Pūjya Guruji Swami Tejomayananda, the talks of many senior Ācāryas like Swami Swaroopananda, Swami Ishwarananda, Swami Nikhilananda, and Swami Abhedananda are available in Mission centers.

Besides the audio recordings brought out by CCMT Publications, a whole range of recordings are done in various Mission centers in India and abroad. Any time jñāna yajñas are conducted, the talks are recorded and made available to the devotees locally. Sometimes the talks are ready on the counter the very next day. Swamini Vimalananda marvels at the efficiency with which it is done in Nairobi under the initiative of Sanjay Soni.

"My yajña ended at 8:30 P.M. and the entire set of talks was available by 9:00! In fact, they had set up the facility at the venue for the audience to download on the spot any talk they wanted on their pen drive."

Early Video Recordings

As early as 1952, at the Pune yajña, Swamiji had been filmed in the yajñaśālā. It is indeed a matter of wonder that, in those days when the film industry was in its infancy, someone had thought of capturing images of a spiritual master in action. It shows how dynamic and dramatic Swamiji was in the yajñaśālā. Further, it also gives us an idea of how inventive Swamiji was in using different media to reach out to the people. In a letter to his cousin Bhaskara Menon, he sends instructions to circulate the film: "Chinmaya wants this to travel all around."

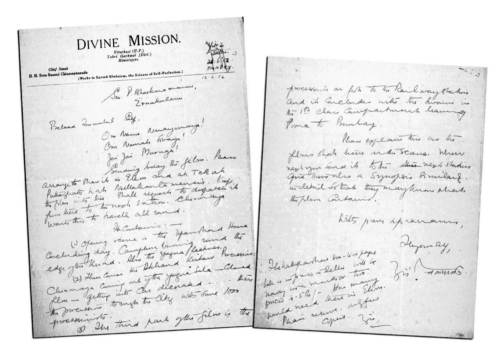

Sending today the film. Please arrange to show it in Ernakulam and at TCR at Puthezhath and at Neelakanta Menon's. Keep the film with thee. Shall request to despatch it from there to the next station. Chinmaya wants this to travel all round.

It contains:

1. Opening scene is the Upanishad Homa concluding day. Camphor burning around the edge of the kund. Also the yagna lectures.

2. Then comes the Akhand Kirtan Procession. Chinmaya coming out of the yagnasala — coloured film — getting into the car decorated ... then the procession through the city with some 1,000 processionists.

3. The third part of the film is the procession on foot to the railway station and it concludes with the Swami in the 1st class compartment leaving Poona to Bombay.

Please explain this as the film shot then on the scene. When next you send it to the next station, give them also a synopsis similarly in detail so that they may know what the film contains.

Pūjya Gurudev's first visit to the U.S. sparked off a tremendous amount of interest. In 1971, Jorge-Luis Jauregui met Gurudev and was so inspired that he wanted to record the talks and share them with others. Ten talks on the third chapter of the *Bhagavad-gītā* and the *Kaivalyopaniṣad* were recorded by him, but unfortunately, they were stolen from his car a few years later.

After that first yajña he had attended, Jorge-Luis got in touch with Rudite Emir, and a Vedānta Study Group was organized at her home in San Francisco, and this functioned fruitfully for many years. About the recordings, Jorge-Luis recalls:

From time to time, during Gurudev's talks, I was assigned to tend to the audio recording of his classes. These were done on a Reel-to-Reel Sony recorder. Later on, my good friend and fellow student, Bill Sheldon, asked me to speak to Gurudev to find out if he would allow us to video-record his talks. Accordingly, I requested Gurudev's permission. He was silent for a minute, and then said, "Go ahead." Since Chinmaya Mission West was not formally organized at that time, Bill got the expensive equipment (an open-reel half inch video tape recorder and camera), and my job was to provide the media (blank videotape reels). This is how the video recordings of Gurudev's talks started.

Later on, when CMW was created, new and better equipment was obtained with funds provided from CMW's financial resources. After that, the various centers or places where Gurudev went to hold *Gītā* Jñāna Yajñas obtained their own equipment. The CMW Publications, run by Nalini Browning, stored and distributed the videos produced.

A few years before he passed away, Bill Sheldon gave me the recorded tapes and the equipment used in the course of the early seventies. I kept them stored carefully for many years. Then, one day, I realized that the tapes were just getting old and may deteriorate on the shelf, so I decided to transfer the reel-to-reel content to what was then a workable format — VHS and BETA — and stored them again.

More years passed, and the VHS and BETA copies sat again on a shelf, getting old, and the digital era had begun. I learned how to convert them to digital format, and years later, I uploaded the videos to YouTube. Since then, those recordings have been and are still being listened to and viewed by many thousands of spiritual seekers.

In July 1974, Pūjya Gurudev gave an interview for the New Heaven–New Earth WCVB Television program hosted by Hubert Jessup. The topic was the 'Teachings of the *Bhagavad Gītā*.' It was recorded in a monastery in Cohasset, Massachusetts. The Rangaswami family arranged for the interview, and the chanting was done in the studio by Leela Rangaswami (who became Swamini Pavitrananda later) and her sister Indra Rangaswami. In recent years, after a relentless search, Mimi Robins located Hubert Jessup, retrieved the recording, and converted it into a DVD. Thus, Chinmaya Mission Boston is the source of this valuable DVD. The publications wing of CCMT is distributing it to the public far and wide.

In 1980, Chuck Schutz, who was already involved in the black-and-white video recordings together with Bill Sheldon, suggested that someone should accompany Swamiji and videotape his lectures, both in the U. S. and in India. Dr. AppaRao Mukkamala supported the idea and offered to buy the equipment needed. It was proposed that Brni. Vilasini (later, Ācārya Vilasini Balakrishnan) should travel with Gurudev and record his talks, and Swamiji gave it the green signal. Chuck taught her to operate the VCR. With a footlocker trunk packed with blank tapes, and a carry-on bag packed with the VCR, tripod, and batteries, she went to India in September 1981. The Indian customs were reluctant to let her through with the trunk full of blank cassettes, but with letters from CCMT and CMW, they allowed her and the equipment into India, recording it in her passport so that she would have to carry the same amount back.

> I clearly remember a brief but piercing moment during a meeting with Gurudev in Krishnalaya. We were telling Gurudev the details about the latest audio-video-taping activities, when he said something like, "Pffft! You cannot learn Vedānta from tapes!" Without stopping even a moment to think, I said vehemently, "But, Swamiji, we *must* continue taping!" Then, as though thunderstruck, I stopped, realizing what he had meant by his words. I smiled, nodding my head as understanding dawned. Of course, true transmission can take place only from one living person to another.
>
> – Rudite Emir

For the next nine months, Vilasini traveled with Gurudev and taped almost all his yajñas in VHS NTSC format, which was generally used in the U.S., but not in India. The tripod was shaky, the lighting variable, and cameras then did not work well in low light. The quality of the tapes was not very good. Gurudev was at first quite happy about the videos and watched with great interest the replays through a tiny monitor and earphones. However, there was a general concern that the recordings were not of professional quality that could be mass produced. Yet all agreed that it was crucial to preserve Gurudev's talks in whichever way possible.

Dr. AppaRao Mukkamala took the initiative to make copies and offer them for sale. Surendra and Kusum Patel handled all the duplicating and marketing on behalf of Chinmaya Publications West. Many of those early yajñas recorded in NTSC format were later digitized thanks to the efforts of Pat and Sagar Loganathan, who edited the material and improved their quality, thus preserving the precious talks and making them available for sale.

In 1982, Vilasini was given a better camera, microphone, and tripod, and was sent off to India again to tape in PAL format, which is used in India. Since these tapes were to be left in India, other Indian devotees helped to bring a few JVC cassettes to India, each one bringing as many as were allowed by the customs authorities. Vilasini remembers those days in vivid detail:

> I would usually sit in the front row of the audience to capture good pictures. At every yajña, I had to reach a day earlier to help the stage crew set up appropriate lighting. It was very difficult to get the right lighting, which would render a good picture, yet not glare in Gurudev's eyes or cause too much heat for him. At almost every location, sincere stage crew members would say, "The first day it may not be all right, but by the second day it will be perfect!"

Gurudev did not like the fuss around the video lights and camera, and would often stop the recording if he didn't think it was going well enough. Some people gave him the feedback that the quality was not up to the mark. Still, with the support of a few others, I persisted and videotaped every yajña, with hopes and prayers that it would be useful for posterity. The best recordings were in Sidhbari, where the entire *Vivekacūḍāmaṇi* was taped, along with other programs, satsaṅgas, and the brahmacārī dīkṣā ceremony.

▲ *Pūjya Gurudev watches the camp delegates preparing to perform an outdoor pūjā in Sidhbari. Vilasini is standing nearby with her camera.*

Vilasini at work with her ▶ video camera

Once, during the recording of a morning class, on a text that had not yet been recorded, the lights burned a fuse. It was the third day of the talks. I continued and recorded the sound and a shadowy picture of Gurudev that came through. That morning, Gurudev told me that I should stop recording the text, since one of the talks was ruined. But I was determined to complete the recording of those talks. I had to get Gurudev's approval somehow before the next morning. So every time I met him — at lunch, in the afternoon, at dinner — I kept trying to get his permission. "Please, Swamiji, this is the only time you will be teaching this text in the whole year," I pleaded. "Lighting was bad only for half an hour," I tried to reason. Every argument I gave was dismissed by Gurudev, who was getting visibly annoyed.

I was desperate and at my wit's end. At 5 o'clock the next morning, during dictation with Gurudev before his morning talk, I made a final bid. The idea had occurred to me during my meditation. With quiet conviction, I told him, "Swamiji, there must be something in my ego that is preventing Swamiji from allowing this recording. Please don't let my ego get in the way of recording this text for future generations!" Swamiji looked at me and finally gave the nod. Absolutely thrilled and relieved, I rushed to set up the camera. The lighting was fine for the rest of the yajña.

The light and sound enactment of *Kamba Rāmāyaṇa* in Madras was a spectacular show with several elaborate stages spread across a huge field, but the night-time, outdoor lighting was not sufficient for good quality recording. I remember lying in the field, out in the dark, trying to get the best view of the different stages. And Manthara almost tripped over my camera while running toward the next stage!

In August 1984, Gurudev held a month-long camp in Krishnalaya, California (called Sandeepany West then), and taught the entire *Bhagavad-gītā*, conducting four classes a day throughout the month. It was a marvelous camp. Lalit Kapoor bought a better camera and mikes, and we arranged for Joy Von Tiedemann, a professional photographer, to help in the videography. I did much of the recording that month. There were many snags — the Chyks[9] in charge of the sound system had problems, and my sound was fed through the sound system instead of through my own external mike. Still, all the talks during the whole month were recorded. Cutaway shots were recorded as well, directed by Jim Coffin. Swamiji complied obediently, humoring everyone, and followed Jim's directions to come in and out of doors, in and out of his kuṭiyā, and walk across the āśrama to the lecture hall, so that these shots could be used for the video introductions. These recordings were compiled and duplicated for sale. A popular audio recording of the *Gītā* was also taken from this camp.

Kamal Bhavnani did some recordings in the VHS format in 1983–84; prominent among them were *Kaṭhopaniṣad, Kaivalyopaniṣad, Ātma Bodha, Logic of Religion,* and *Sādhana Pañcakam,* which was titled 'Values of Life.' Asha Kamdar recalls:

> Kamal turned out amazing work with just one of those cameramen, who do the video shooting at weddings. She insisted that he stand around with the camera wherever Gurudev was, even at informal satsaṅgas during the 1986 *Bhagavad-gītā* camp in Sidhbari. Because of that, we have today a lot of material other than the lectures. There was one satsaṅga in the open courtyard outside Gurudev's kuṭiyā, where some army officers from the Yol

---

9   Members of Chinmaya Yuva Kendra

camp had gathered and asked questions. Gurudev talked about Buddha, and about Dalai Lama. Those were precious recordings.

As for Gurudev, the harsh lights for the video cameras must have been difficult to endure. The glare and the heat were obviously causing a lot of distress. When a devotee remarked on it, he simply shrugged it aside and said, "After a few years, this is all you will have." Through all the hustle and bustle, he maintained his poise, his perspective, and his vision. Once, when the noise of the fans and other equipment was becoming very intrusive and causing a lot of distraction, he simply said, "Think of it as the roar of the Ganges in the background." With a simple shift of perspective, he could get the message across.

In 1991, Isabel Taylor created a landmark of sorts by recording the entire set of talks on the *Bhagavad-gītā* delivered by Pūjya Gurudev at Krishnalaya in Piercy, California. This was done professionally by Bradley Boatman, a well-known producer with twenty years of experience. Let us hear the story directly from her:

I traveled around India with Swamiji for a few weeks in 1989 after my first meeting with him, attended all his talks, and basked in His presence. I bought several of his books. I was appalled at the poor quality of the manufacturing of his books and videos with the exception of the *Mananam* booklets, which were splendid. I asked him how a teacher as great as he could have books with so many mistakes and typos, and how the videos could be of such poor quality. I said, "A great teacher deserves great books and videos for posterity!"

After that, wherever we went, when someone asked him about making videos, he would point to me and say, "She's making them in America!" I tried to explain I did not know anything about video production or book publishing. Nevertheless, Swamiji continued saying to all who asked that I would be making them in America.

After six wonderful weeks of traveling with Him, I left India. A few months later, I received a call from Vilasini in Washington, D.C., who had received a letter from Swamiji asking her to contact me for help with the editing of his publications! I explained to her that I had no experience with editing, publishing, or video production, but that I would be happy to help in any way I could.

In October 1990, I visited India again and traveled with him for a few months, during which he continued saying I would make the videos in America. When I returned to the United States, I began searching in earnest for a good producer. After interviewing several people, I chose Bradley Boatman, who was highly recommended. And Swamiji endorsed the choice.

Bradley Boatman started preparing a crew, rented top-quality cameras, and went to Piercy to see the place and meet the people. Together, with a representative of the board of Chinmaya Mission West, I signed a contract with Bradley Boatman, and we worked out the costs, timing, and other details. It was to be a major project, nearing $100,000 in cost.

Despite the challenges of finding the means to finance such a significant project, and my own lack of experience in the video production field, Bhagavān had told me he wanted to sing His song, and so I proceeded.

Chinmaya Mission West provided me with its mailing list, and I had a beautiful pamphlet made about the *Gītā* to be produced at Piercy, California, the following June (1991). I mailed the pamphlet to all Chinmaya Mission members, offering a discount on the videotapes for anyone who preordered the video set of about forty hours. More than seventy people who wanted to support Swamiji's work sent in preorders, and the cost of the project began to appear reachable.

▲ *Bradley Boatman, the producer, is on the extreme right, next to Anjali Browning in a saree. Janine and three cameramen complete the crew of the production team at Piercy, California.*

Janine at work behind the camera ▶

In April, I returned to Sidhbari to be with Swamiji. One day, as he was leaving the dining hall, he said to me: "I am taking an Indian crew to film the *Gītā* at the same time. My people need to have access to this, too." I remember exclaiming vehemently to Him: "We are *all* your people, Swamiji!" And I typed him a long letter saying that his will be done, not mine. In the end, Swamiji decided to go with the original film crew, with the assurance that the NTSC master video could be converted to the

PAL system used in India. After the videos were made, I had a set of master tapes made in PAL format. I gave them to the Central Chinmaya Mission Trust to ensure that copies could be made for all of Swamiji's followers in the subcontinent — Europe, Asia, Australia, and anywhere the PAL video format was used.

Checks for preordering the videotapes kept coming in, and by June 1, 1991, the first day of the *Bhagavad-gītā* videotaping, we had enough to finance the whole project. However, I had to leave within a few days, as my first granddaughter was born in Portugal! When I was saying goodbye to Swamiji, someone asked me, "After so many months of preparation for these videos, how can you leave after just a few days of filming?" I replied, "It is Swamiji's project, not mine!" Swamiji exclaimed, "She is detached, you see!"

▲ *Pūjya Gurudev giving discourses on* Bhagavad-Gītā *at Krishnalaya in Piercy, California, in 1984*

Later, I joined Swamiji in Montreal, where Bradley Boatman had sent a cassette, which Swamiji and I saw together. I liked the quality very much, but was appalled at all the titles given to everyone on the board of CMW, even myself. I told Bradley to take all those names off, as well as our thanks to Gurudev. Who were we to thank him? The professional staff did receive recognition, as was their due. A month later, another cassette came with the acknowledgments reduced to the professional staff, who did such superb work, but it said, "This production would not have been possible without the participation of all the members of Chinmaya Mission, as I had told him to put, but there was also added: especially Isabel Taylor."

I called Bradley Boatman, who told me Vilasini had discussed it with Swamiji, and it was he who wanted my name in the video credits. I went to him angrily: "Swamiji, why did you do this to me? I want to get rid of my ego, not boost it!" He replied, "Yes, in your heart you know it was all His work, but you were a major part of the production team, and I wanted you to be listed."

While still in Montreal, I requested Swamiji to give an introduction to the *Bhagavad-gītā* videos. It took some doing to convince him, but he finally agreed. It was called *The Logic of Spirituality*. This introduction itself became very popular. The introduction and each chapter were available separately, as they are even today.

In early January of 1992, I took the PAL master copies to the Chinmaya Mission in Bombay and stayed with Asha Kamdar and her wonderful mother, Pushpa Kamdar. Swamiji had decided that Asha would be the one to manage and direct Chinmaya Mission's videos in all its aspects.

swami chinmayananda

CHINMAYA TAPOVAN TRUST, SANDEEPANY HIMALAYAS, SIDHBARI-176057, H.P. INDIA, PHONE: 01892-2121/2251.

30 December 1991

Smt Isabel Taylor
c/o Sri Narain Bhatia
CCMT Sandeepany Sadhanalaya
Powai Park Drive
Bombay 400 072

Blessed Self:

Hari Om! Hari Om! Hari Om!
Salutations!

Yours of 9th December has just reached me here in Sidhabari.

There is nothing special to write except that you are welcome to this spiritual centre.

While you are there, meet Asha Kamdar and discuss about the tapes. I have requested her to take charge of advertising and distributing the Geeta tapes. She will be entirely all in all In-charge of it. She has got a team of teen-agers to help her and her residence will be our Video Tapes Centre.

Let her make the necessary letter-heads, receipt books, etc. Call it :

GEETA   TAPES   CENTRE

**(Video-tapes Department of Central Chinmaya
Mission Trust, Powai, Bombay 400 072)**

If necessary, take a couple of days to discuss with Asha and then come away.

With Prem and Om,

Thy Own Self,

CHINMAYA

Then I traveled to Sidhbari to see Swamiji. I was so happy that, as he came out of his room, I just hugged him and he hugged me in joy. He said to me, "You have been polished many times through this process, and you have learned much. And the others have also learned something: not to mess with you! Hahaha ...."

Several months later, as I was traveling with Swamiji in Singapore, he told us he would be giving a three-month series of talks on the *Vivekacūḍāmaṇi* in Sidhbari in the fall. Again, the thought came: Why not record that as well?

I discussed this with Swamiji, who at first said that hiring a professional team for three months would be too expensive. Brni. Arpita (now Swamini Radhikananda) of the U. S. and I decided to contribute, and with the generous donation of Ms. Rajpriya Bukory from Mauritius, we came up with the necessary funds. When I presented him with the proposed budget and Shubhra Tandon's name, as well as that of Asha Kamdar, and told him about the funding, he said, "Well, all right, go ahead."

▲ *Isabel Taylor (left) and Rajpriya Bukory (right) with Pūjya Gurudev*

Those three months of the *Vivekacūḍāmaṇi* talks were magical. More than 500 people attended and each one felt it. It was a wonderful parting gift to us all, for he attained Mahāsamādhi on August 3, 1993.

Rudite Emir shared a very interesting story about an entirely different video venture with Gurudev:

In the summer of 1992, it was decided to create a movie at Krishnalaya, not the usual kind (such as a video of one of Gurudev's lectures or satsaṅgas), but a movie with a plot. The inspiration for this was David Jones, master of aerial camerawork, who had been acting as the aerial director of Hollywood movies for more than twenty years. Having befriended the Browning family, he ended up at Krishnalaya and became deeply devoted to Gurudev.

During one of his visits to Krishnalaya, Jones arrived in his beloved helicopter. After giving joyful rides to any camp attendee who dared climb into his helicopter, the beginnings were forged of a movie plot featuring Gurudev, an actress, and David Jones as the helicopter pilot. Jones was also the movie director and cameraman.

The setting for the movie was a tiny island on the Eel River, which borders the Krishnalaya property. I was conscripted to play an executive. The ambitious executive's office was represented by a desk hauled out mid-river onto the island, with a decorative rug in front of it. Besides the desk, the production details were very few: a hat for the executive, a pile of papers on the desk to signify the load of work and, of course, the helicopter.

The plot was simple: An ambitious woman executive is fully entrenched in her ego-driven work at the desk when along comes Gurudev riding in a helicopter piloted by Jones. As Gurudev rides

▲ *Movie director David Jones gives directives to Rudite. Anjali Browning is in the background, assisting.*

▲ *Gurudev flies by in a helicopter.*

by, with the helicopter swinging low over the desk, he shouts out a message to the executive to open her heart and mind to the true meaning of life. Though taken by surprise, the executive hears every word relayed to her, allows the message of Vedānta to sink deep into her being, and strews the pile of work documents into the air.

▲ *The lady lets the papers fly as Gurudev's message sinks in.*

After measuring the light, setting up the equipment, and giving the actress directions on how to proceed, Director Jones took off in his helicopter, with Gurudev sitting in the seat next to him. The helicopter swooped down frighteningly close to the desk, creating such a wind that the executive had no trouble letting all her papers fly. Meanwhile, Gurudev was laughing his deep, infectious laugh as he leaned out of the helicopter window, enjoying every moment of the show.

Soon thereafter, a severe illness took David Jones from this world, and the envisioned movie was never completed, though a short draft version of it exists.

Chinmaya Darshanam

Chinmaya Darshanam was the name given to the DVD project and some of the audio projects undertaken by Chinmaya Publications West (CPW), which archived all the recorded material of the various lectures over the years. These recordings of Pūjya Gurudev were mostly made by Vilasini Balakrishnan, Kusum Patel, and other devotees over a period of many years. Swami Siddhananda, who heads CPW and is in charge of these precious materials, was concerned that the recordings might deteriorate if they continued to be stored in the form that they were in. In October 2002, Swamiji asked Dr. Sagar Loganathan and other devotees to see if they could digitize and archive the material.

The project, which started as an archiving attempt, became a DVD and CD reproduction program. Swami Siddhananda provided all the assistance and the equipment needed by the team. Gradually, Dr. Loganathan familiarized himself with the computerized video editing technology, which was in its infancy then. Their first attempt was 'Satsaṅg with Gurudev — Q & A at Olivette, Michigan,' which took four months to finish. It was a simple DVD, not requiring menus. Later, the Upaniṣad series was made interactive, so that the mantras could be accessed individually.

Additional equipment for copying and printing was bought for the project, and they ventured into commercial production. Pat Loganathan was involved in designing the covers and printing the discs. The demand grew, especially during the camp season, when thousands of discs were needed. Śrī Bipin and Smt. Brinda Bhat, senior devotees who had been reproducing audio-cassettes for Swamiji, agreed to take over the production part of the project and have been carrying the tremendous load ever since. During the 2008 Mahāsamādhi Camp at Rocky Gap, Maryland, the last of Gurudev's lecture series was ready for sale, and Swami Tejomayananda officially released the *Rāma Gītā* DVD series to the public. For a complete list of DVDs and audio CDs, please visit www.chinmayapublication.com.

Chinmaya Video Dham

Chinmaya Video Dham in India began in July 1991, with the set of master tapes of the *Bhagavad-gītā* recording in Piercy, sent by Isabel Taylor. Pūjya Gurudev put Asha Kamdar in charge of the whole project and instructed that all audio and video recordings be collected and sent to her. Preparing new recordings and distributing them was also entrusted to Asha and her team, who worked from her residence, which doubled up as the office.

The first recording that Chinmaya Dham did was a talk by Gurudev on 'Ecology — The Modern Confusion,' delivered at K. C. College, Mumbai. Next was the major task of recording the *Vivekacūḍāmaṇi* talks in Sidhbari in 1992. Shubhra Tandon was the director, and a team of twenty people consisting of cameramen, lighting technicians, attendants, and so on, went with her to Sidhbari to do the recording from July 28 to October 10.

In November 1992, Swami Tejomayananda conducted a Bhāgavata Saptāha at the Birla Krida Kendra, in Chowpatty. Pūjya Gurudev gave an introductory talk there. The entire saptāha was recorded in video mode.

After Gurudev's Mahāsamādhi, in December 1994, Swami Tejomayananda conducted a mahā yajña in Hindi at Azad Nagar in Mumbai and covered all eighteen chapters of the *Gītā* in eighteen days. In the mornings, he talked on the Upaniṣads, eight of them altogether. Asha and her team worked very hard editing and preparing the master copy immediately so that they could present the audio as well as the video recordings of both the *Gītā* and the Upaniṣad talks for sale the very next day.

The work expanded, and in 1995 they had to move out, because they were working out of a residential complex and neighbors objected to the heavy traffic of people, and to the heavy cartons going in and out. So the team moved to a rented place nearby. Asha bought some secondhand equipment, because it was cumbersome and also expensive to borrow the equipment. Furthermore, when it was not in use, she rented it out to take care of the overhead expenses like telephone and electricity.

In 1997, they moved again to a commercial complex in Kharghar, near the Central Station. The year 2000–2001 saw very hectic activity in the Video Dham, as all the Mission centers and other units wanted to make their own documentaries for the Vishwa Sammelan, the fiftieth anniversary celebrations of Chinmaya Mission, to be held in Mumbai in December 2001. A lot of material was available in Chinmaya Video Dham, and so everyone flocked there. "It was like a year-long melā [festival gathering]," recalls Asha, as she explains the history further:

> In the meantime, Neela Kapadia, a filmmaker, whose father Kakubhai Kapadia had also done some films for the Mission in the 1960s and 70s, was commissioned by Swami Tejomayananda to make a film on Chinmaya Mission. She did the film editing in the Video Dham. She wanted me to go with their unit for the extensive shooting. We went to Delhi, where we rented a bus. There was Neela, with one cameraman, one sound recorder, Kusum Patel's son, and me. We traveled past Haridwar and Rishikesh, and reached Uttarkashi at midnight. Swami Dhyanananda wouldn't open the gates. We had to knock repeatedly, call out and persuade him from outside.
>
> We did some of the shooting in Tapovan Maharaj's kuṭiyā [cottage] and outside, and then went to Gangotri. Swami Sundarananda allowed us to do some shooting inside Tapovan Maharaj's kuṭiyā there. He showed us the place where Gurudev, as a disciple, used to prepare the food for Swami Tapovan Maharaj.

In the late 1990s, we used to make the recordings in VHS format, eight copies at a time. VCDs and DVDs were new to us. As I browsed through our collection, I noticed some close-up shots with different expressions here and there. It occurred to me that we could bring all those close-ups together and make some kind of a film. I tried doing it myself several times, but it didn't work out.

As the work increased, we hired a full-time editor, a young boy called Bhavesh Thakur, who was a professional, but had a spiritual streak. I told him of my dream, indicating all the master tapes stacked on the blue racks. There was another young man, Apoorva Saxena, who had a photographic memory of what was in which tape. He and Bhavesh worked together for 15–20 days. Then they called me inside to have a look at what they had done. They had made a very nice montage, but it was barely two-and-a-half minutes. They said they were going to work along those lines. They collected about 1,000 visuals, but finally chose only 350 of them. It was a nineteen-and-a-half minute film. Bhavesh had captured Gurudev moving from sunrise to sunset, meditating, walking, and laughing — *Many Moods of the Master*!

Then the music had to be put together with a music arranger. We called Darshan Kanhar. Himanshu Nanda played the flute and picked up some verses for chanting. Tabla, sitar, and violin were live. We didn't want a keyboard. We rented the Bloom Studio in Mahim. Our VHS cassette was played in this recording room and each instrumentalist was added separately. The stream was there. They were told to look at it and play whatever they wanted to play. Each track was recorded separately. Finally, we did a mix and slapped it on. Then we came back and played it in our studio. But still something was missing.

Next door was an audio studio, belonging to Pratap Sharma. His sound recorder was a very dear friend of mine called Vijay. So I called him up for help. We took our dry tracks to his studio; he did a mix in his computer and slapped it on. The whole thing came alive.

We wanted the film to be dedicated to Gurudev at his Samādhi in Sidhbari. Everybody who was involved in making the film — twelve of us, to be precise — went to Sidhbari by train. Kalidas, who is full of stories about Gurudev, was also there and Bhavesh spent all his time with him, wanting to hear more about Gurudev. Bhavesh would have tears in his eyes and remark, "Why was I not born twenty years earlier!"

On August 2, 2001, we set up everything in the old Satsang Hall. Speakers, amplifiers, and wires everywhere, adjusted to get the best possible sound effects. It took us half a day, from the afternoon till 8 o'clock in the evening. No one wanted to eat dinner. We were all nervous, not knowing what would be the reaction to the film.

The show started at 9:00 P.M. Swami Tejomayananda was among the audience. I had with me a youngster who had started off as a light man for weddings, a Marathi boy, who could not speak English. Later, he worked in a studio, where he learned how to edit. He used to come over to help us after his work. He would stay on till late at night and then go to sleep in the room itself — our house was a free-for-all. They would come and work, and make themselves at home. This boy positioned himself behind one of the pillars to capture Swami Tejomayananda's reaction to the film.

When the film was over, there was pin-drop silence. Swami Tejomayananda's eyes were welling up with tears, and he quietly started walking away. And this boy continued shooting, walking backward, recording the expression on Swamiji's face. Finally, it was clear that everybody loved it; everyone was deeply moved by the film. *Many Moods of the Master* was screened on the first day of the Vishwa Sammelan in December 2001.

In the meantime, in September 2001, Swami Tejomayananda wanted to record the entire *Rāmacaritmānas* in different rāgas. Audio recording was done at Anupama Studios in Andheri every morning from 7:30 to 9:30. We started on September 1st and finished on the 28th. Bharati Ganatra's mother used to send breakfast for us to the studio. Bharati and I did the editing, pausing in the right places. Cover designs were done by Durga Singh. Copies were made in cassettes and CDs. It was released during the Vishwa Sammelan.

We continued our work after that by making CDs and DVDs of various talks. Gurudev's *Vivekacūḍāmaṇi* was on VCDs, and we wanted to convert them into DVDs. There were a total of 107 lectures. Despite compacting them into double layers, it took a total of 34 DVDs. We made it interactive. I am not very good at doing such things. A young man called Rahul Jhaveri was recommended to me and helped me with the job. He was good at everything — hardware, software, and editing. He took 8–9 months to do it. We prepared a booklet with the verses to go with the DVD set.

After that, we worked on the *Kaṭhopaniṣad* and Rahul Jhaveri made a beautiful montage. Even though he was from the film industry and we paid him at the market rates, he did not approach our work like a commercial film; he had a feeling for it and would dive into the talks to catch their spirit.

When Jeevan Darshan was being set up in Chinmaya Vibhooti, Durga Singh, Bharati Sukhatankar, and I worked together to categorize the question-and-answer clips. A visitor could click on a question and get Gurudev's answer in his own voice.

In 2007, I told Swami Tejomayananda that I would like to retire in three years' time and asked him to give me someone whom I could train. He never took me seriously. Finally, during the Sevaks' Camp, I announced my resignation and M. Santhosh took over.

Chinmaya Video Dham was moved to the premises of the Sandeepany Sadhanalaya in Mumbai and Yuva Veer M. Santhosh took charge of the Chinmaya Video Dham for the next couple of years. Slowly a new team was created, and high-end digital equipment was purchased. Today, a team of six professionals are doing excellent work, coordinating with the other wings of Chinmaya Mission like the IT team, various Mission centers, and Ācāryas.

Talks by Pūjya Guruji Swami Tejomayananda are recorded to be produced as professional quality DVDs and marketed with help from Sony. Old recordings of Pūjya Gurudev in spools and cassettes are cleaned up and retrieved. Good quality material is converted to DVDs, and some of the talks are uploaded to the Chinmaya Channel on YouTube, where they continue to attract thousands of viewers. About 500–600 hours of talks by Pūjya Gurudev have been cleaned and converted from analog tapes to digital format.

Now, talks by other Ācāryas, such as Swami Swaroopananda, are also being produced commercially. Archiving discourses by Ācāryas, lectures of the Vedānta Course in Mumbai, programs of Chinmaya Naada Bindu, and major functions of the Chinmaya Mission are some of the aspects of work done by the Chinmaya Video Dham.

Publicity material is created for the various projects of Chinmaya Mission. Short clips of 15–20 minutes are prepared for the Chinmaya Sanchar app. Videos are prepared for download through iTunes. The focus is on expanding the reach through Internet and multimedia channels. After all, Pūjya Gurudev wanted the message to reach as many people as possible.

PART FOUR

LEAVES, BUDS, AND FLOWERS

ॐ

Leaves, Buds, and Flowers

Magazines for All Ages

Chinmaya Mission centers around the world publish many periodicals and magazines, each catering to the specific interests of a category of readers. Some address a broad readership, others focus on specific age groups, and many relay updates on Chinmaya Mission events in addition to providing inspiring articles on Vedānta.

Tapovan Prasad is the principal magazine of Chinmaya Mission and enjoys worldwide readership. It carries thought-provoking articles by the Ācāryas of Mission centers in India and abroad, accounts of satsaṅgas with the Chinmaya Guru Paramparā, summarized reports of Mission activities all over the globe, and announcements of upcoming events. *Balvihar* magazine is meant exclusively for children, while *Chinmaya Udghosh* addresses and inspires the youth. *Vanprasth* deals with lifestyle issues that relate to senior citizens. We shall take a brief look at each of these magazines and a few other publications individually.

◀ Swami Siddhananda with the three editors: (L to R) Rukma Naik (Chinmaya Udghosh), *Swamini Aaradhanananda* (Balvihar), *Parvathy Raman* (Tapovan Prasad)

Tapovan Prasad

Tapovan Prasad came into being in January 1963, the same month that saw the opening of the Sandeepany Sadhanalaya in Bombay (now Mumbai). The first issue was dated December 31, 1962, but by the end of 1963, the date was corrected to denote the first of every month. It has remained the flagship magazine of Chinmaya Mission for more than fifty years, publishing articles by Gurudev Swami Chinmayananda, Guruji Swami Tejomayananda, and other dynamic Ācāryas to inspire and guide seekers all over the world.

The importance and value of the magazine can be gauged from the fact that it has been a trusted resource of historical material for almost all the books in this special Mananam Centenary Series. Many of the articles first serialized in *Tapovan Prasad* have later been published in book form.

The magazine's 'Mission News' section has faithfully recorded the major events in Chinmaya Mission, thus providing an authentic historical timeline for posterity. This section keeps the global Chinmaya family connected and abreast of all the happenings.

Tapovan Prasad also provides the most comprehensive list of major upcoming events worldwide. Many are the readers who have responded to a camp announcement and proceeded to discover the magic world of spiritual camaraderie that changed their lives forever.

After the first five years, the magazine moved from Bombay (now Mumbai) to Madras (now Chennai) and Smt. Leela Nambiar became the publisher from June 1968. She has continued to be the backbone of the magazine for almost five decades, often officiating as the editor when the need arose. Pūjya Gurudev brought up the magazine lovingly, nourishing it with valuable inputs in the form of articles and letters, encouraging and guiding the editors, and personally canvassing for subscriptions.

Tapovan Prasad Editors Through the Years

December	62	- December	64	: Swami Dayananda
January	65	- May	68	: A. Parthasarathy
June	68	- October	70	: Leela Nambiar
November	70	- May	73	: T. Rajagopalan
June	73	- July	73	: Leela Nambiar
September	73	- September	75	: V. Damodara Menon
October	75	- December	75	: Leela Nambiar
January	76	- March	76	: N. Ramanathan
April	76			: Leela Nambiar
May	76	- July	81	: Viji Sundaram
August	81	- January	82	: G.L. Mohan
February	82	- March	82	: Leela Nambiar
March	82	- October	94	: C. Ammini Kutty
November	94	- December	97	: G. Sriramulu
January	98	- March	02	: Swamini Niranjanananda
April	02	- till date		: Parvathy Raman

In January 1974, when *Tapovan Prasad* completed eleven years, Pūjya Gurudev sent a message which was published in the magazine.

Gurudev's Gift and Greetings for the New Year

MESSAGE

To look back is healthy, if we use the past to plan intelligently the present for making the future glorious achievement.

By now Tapovan Prasad has served the Chinmaya community of seekers for eleven years. To day Tapovan Prasad is no more a spiritual journal meant for our Indian groups, but it has become an Internationally-read magazine for all Hindu spiritual seekers. We have readers in all the continents, and soon we may have to start publishing it in different languages.

I am especially mentioning this idea to emphasize, the need for a new vision both in the Editorial Board and in the writers. Too much of Technical expressions may be avoided, and carefully use footnotes or parenthetical clauses, to explain vividly the Sanskrit terms so that our friends outside India can clearly grasp the full significance of the philosophical thought.

News of our foreign centres must also find place in Tapovan Prasad now and I request all our Chinmaya Family groups out side India to report once a month to the Editor, Tapovan Prasad, the summary of your activities in your group. Of course this will perhaps create a painful reaction. Our centres in foreign lands may get floods of letters, from wandering-masters from India. But our standing instruction will help you all. No centre can accept anyone directly approaching the centre unless he has received a clearance letter from Central Chinmaya Mission Trust Secretary, Sri Ram Batra. This will guarantee the genuineness of the preacher reaching your centres.

We must improve our quality of production: paper, printing techniques of display, cover-page and perhaps make it more pictorial. All these means more funds. This is not a profit-seeking journal. We are making the subscription minimum, and are taking in a few advertisements, just to meet our humble budget. The only way it can be an honourable and decent journal is by the subscribers themselves. If each one of you can persuade another to try Tapovan Prasad for a year or if each one of you can gift away to some one, friend or relation a year's subscription, We shall send our issues with your complements.

Students and others who can not afford to subscribe can earn one year's Tapovan Prasad **free** when you canvass ten subscribers for us.

With such a family-like mutual co-operation and goodwill we shall launch into an year of Greater efforts and larger successes.

May the Blessings of Jagadeeswara be upon us all. May we in the purity of action become fit for greater actions.

Kuwait,
Arabia,
1st January, 1974.

IMPORTANT ANNOUNCEMENT

Due to the very high cost of printing and paper we are forced to increase the price of the " Tapovan Prasad " per copy from 60 ps to 85 ps and to enhance the yearly subscription from Rs. 7 (*Rupees Seven*) to Rs. 10 (*Rupees ten only*) within India and from $ 1 (Rs. 10) to $ 2 (Rs. 15) out side India by Sea Mail. The rate of Annual Subscription by Air Mail will be enhanced from $ 7 (Rs. 50) to $ 10 (Rs. 75)

The above enhanced rates will take effect from the 1st of May 1974. So our esteemed subscribers whose annual subscription for the magazine expires on the 30th April 1974, will have to pay for the renewal at the above rates.

As we are compelled to enhance the above subscription rates due to reasons far beyond our control, we trust and hope that our esteemed subscribers will bear with us and will continue their kind patronage of the Magazine.

Editor.

From Tapovan Prasad, ▶
April 1974

Tapovan Prasad celebrated its golden jubilee in the year 2012 with a special commemorative cover and features recapturing some of its historical highlights. Even though an online version was successfully started, especially for the convenience of the readers abroad, the print version has remained a general favorite.

Announcement published in
▼ Tapovan Prasad, *1969*

CENTRAL CHINMAYA MISSION TRUST
HUMBLY ANNOUNCES "BALA VIHAR"
CHILDREN'S MONTHLY MAGAZINE IN ENGLISH PUBLISHED ON
15TH OF EVERY MONTH

*BALA VIHAR presents you with
Fun & Fantasy for the growing mind
A collection of wits, puzzles and quizzes.
Art & Craft
A collection of do-it-yourself series.
Myths & Folklore
Fables & tales with morals from Puranas, Upanishads, Ramayana, Mahabharatha etc.
History – Glorious past & present
A collection of inspiring personalities, events from History.
Know Your Land & People
Short sketch of places, people, their culture & customs.
Rhymes & Prayers
A collection from Geeta, Vedas & Scriptures.
*BALA VIHAR is yours a full year for Rs. 6/- Only.
*BALA VIHAR first issue starts from November 15, 1969.
*Send your subscription with the form duly filled today itself.
*Use the subscription form inserted in this T. P. issue.

WHAT YOU CAN DO FOR "BALA VIHAR"
THE CHILDREN'S ENGLISH MONTHLY?

1. Send your subscription form and subscription, today itself.
2. Contact your relatives, neighbours and friends to enrol them as subscribers. List of Subscribers, their addresses may be sent instead of subscription form
3. Organise subscription drive in your area/centre to enrol subscribers.
4. If you have a flair for writing, write articles on topics described elsewhere in this issue about "BALAVIHAR"
5. Collect articles on topics mentioned elsewhere in this book from your children/friends and send them to:

The Editor, "Bala Vihar",
Band Box House, 254, Dr. Annie Besant Road,
Prabhadevi Post Office, Bombay-25 (DD)

Please note that the Editor "Bala Vihar" reserves the right either to accept or reject any article. Accepted articles become the property of Central Chinmaya Mission Trust.

Balvihar

The inaugural issue of *Balvihar* magazine, dedicated solely to children, came out in November 1969 from Mumbai. Aruna Sheth was the first editor, and among the editors who followed her were Atul Sukhatankar and Asha Kamdar. In the late 1980s, the publication moved to Chennai, with Thoyajakshi as the editor. In January 1996, the magazine moved back to Mumbai, with Brni. Vividisha Chaitanya (now Swamini

Aaradhanananda) as the editor, and Smt. Bharati Sukhatankar as the editorial advisor. They have continued to serve the magazine wholeheartedly for almost two decades now, increasing the readership of 9,000 to a whopping 40,000 (as on July 15, 2015). "I realized that writing for kids means getting *into* their skin, not *under* their skin! It also means losing oneself in a world of fun, wonder, innocence, and perennial discovery," says Swamini Aaradhanananda.

Balvihar has an international circulation and is now printed in attractive colors with interesting features. Many adults also enjoy reading it. The story of *Balvihar* has been given in more detail in the earlier book in this series, titled *Our Children, Our Future* (pages 99-101).

Chinmaya Udghosh

Chinmaya Udghosh is the monthly magazine of Chinmaya Yuva Kendra, the youth wing of Chinmaya Mission worldwide. It was started by Br. Abhay Chaitanya (now Swami Abhedananda), who had the vision of a magazine, wholly dedicated to the youth, which would include articles that provide practical application of scriptural knowledge, career counseling, useful tips for handling problems of life, motivational poems, discussions on contemporary issues, cartoons, inspirational quotations, as well as articles by Pūjya Gurudev.

In December 1995, the idea for this magazine was presented to Pūjya Guruji Swami Tejomayananda, during his visit to Indore. Later, a detailed proposal was submitted and was approved by him. Br. Abhay Chaitanya chose the name 'Udghosh,' which means a clarion call or announcement of something glorious — the glory of Pūjya Gurudev and his message. He also gave it the motto 'Clarion Call for Dynamic Spirituality.' The first issue of *Chinmaya Udghosh* came out in March 1996.

Started as a bimonthly, the magazine was so successful that it was soon converted to a monthly publication. In December 1997, Pūjya Guruji Swami Tejomayananda announced that *Chinmaya Udghosh* would be the global CHYK magazine, the mouthpiece of Chinmaya Yuva Kendra.

One of the highlights was the coffee-table book called *Crescendo Peaks*, published by *Chinmaya Udghosh* and released during the Chinmaya Vishwa Sammelan in December 2001. For ten successful years, the magazine was produced by members of the Yuva Kendra in Indore. Shiv Kumar Iyer, who was a part of the core team, writes: "The best part about publishing and producing this magazine was the day-to-day proximity with Pūjya Gurudev, his life, work, and vision. Searching for articles and reading a variety of inspirational books to collect material for the magazine enriched us in unexpected ways.

It was a great opportunity for us to work closely as a team, dedicated to a higher cause, bonded by our devotion to Pūjya Gurudev."

In February 2006, the magazine was handed over to AICHYK, (All India Chinmaya Yuva Kendra) to be published under the guidance of Swami Mitrananda, who continues to inspire the editorial team and the young writers who contribute to the magazine. More details about CU, as the magazine has come to be known, as well as other publications by AICHYK, are presented exhaustively in the book titled *Youth Alone Can* (pages 162–184) in this Mananam Series.

Vanprasth

Senior citizens of Chinmaya Mission have a quarterly journal of their own, named *Vanprasth*. It was first published in April 1998 with Swami Shankarananda as the editor. Besides articles on spirituality, it touches upon various concerns of old age and teaches the art of aging gracefully. From the secret of contentment to illustrated exercises, the magazine provides nourishment for the mind

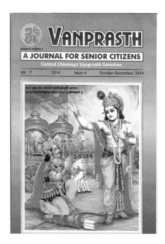

and the body. It continues to be published from Allahabad by Swami Yogasthananda.

The Story of *Mananam*

Mananam, the primary periodical of Chinmaya Mission West, started as a quarterly journal. Pūjya Gurudev mentions *Mananam* as early as 1975, but the first issue of the journal came out only in January 1978. Pūjya Gurudev had instructed the editorial board that the cover of the first issue must carry the picture of Ādi Śaṅkarācārya. This was to be followed by cover pictures of Swami Vivekananda, Swami Sivananda, and Swami Tapovan Maharaj in subsequent issues. After this wisdom lineage was represented, the January 1979 issue carried Pūjya Gurudev's image on the cover, a drawing created especially for *Mananam* by an artist from Sweden.

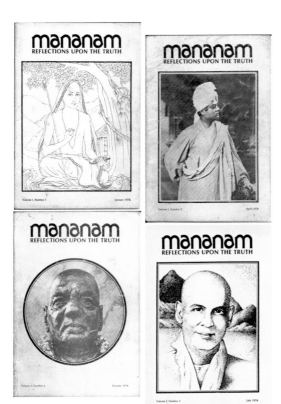

Gurudev assigned Rudite Emir as the first editor. With a dedicated team — Vijay Kapoor, Nalini Browning, Gail Larrick, Ruth Lundgren, Byron Hayes, and others — Rudite brought out the first issue, printed by Family Press of Napa, California, under the able supervision of Bill Browning.

Page 8—INDIA-WEST—March 15, 1978

New Vedanta Journal Launched

In January 1978 appeared the maiden issue of **Mananam**, an elegantly conceived and thoughtfully edited journal on Vedanta. Among the many recently launched American magazines on spiritual or pseudospiritual topics, **Mananam** stands out as a publication with an undiluted purpose: to publish articles on Vedanta--in terms understandable to the Westerner, but without any compromises with the original meaning of the teaching in the Upanishads and the **Bhagavad Gita**.

The quarterly journal is published by Chinmaya Mission (West), a nonprofit corporation and the Western branch of Swami Chinmayananda's renown Chinmaya Mission in India. The goals of the organization are educational: to spread the knowledge of Eastern spiritual thought, in particular Vedanta, and to encourage the application of Vedantic principles in service to the community. The Mission is headquartered in Napa, California, but has regional branches all over North America. **Mananam**'s editorial offices are in San Francisco; its business offices, in Napa.

The inspiration for the publication of **Mananam** was provided by Swami Chinmayananda, who, for the last twenty-five years, has been spear-heading a movement in India to open up to the public at large the knowledge contained in the **Bhagavad Gita** and the Upanishads, something that had been unheard of before his time, when the sacred texts were under the jealous guardianship of the priest class alone. **Mananam** is part of Swami Chinmayananda's work to reach out to the people to answer their inner needs. Already, despite its short existence, **Mananam** has had an overwhelmingly positive response from its reading public.

The editorial board of the journal states its goal thus: to present as clear an expression of Vedantic thought as possible, taking into account the needs of the student in the beginning stages of study, yet being careful not to let the main thrust of Vedanta be diverted by any suggestion of cultism, magical solutions, or pseudospiritual interests.

Four pages in each issue of the 48-page journal are devoted to a section called "Youngsteps," geared specifically to children. It offers stories, poems, sayings, and personal accounts that depict abstract spiritual ideas in concrete images. Many of their topics are taken from Hindu mythology, others are from Western sources. The children's section is profusely illustrated to help relay the abstract ideas to the child's mind. Another special feature of the journal is a continuing series of lessons on Sanskrit.

The journal, a quarterly publi-

In those pre-personal-computer days, *Mananam* was painstakingly created on an electric typewriter that had the extra feature of justifying the right margin. Unlike today, when errors can be corrected with a simple push of the delete or backspace key, every typesetting error and editorial revision had to be physically cut into the reproduction proofs and pasted in without a trace. Once, clutching the sheaf of such just-corrected proofs from the typist's office, Rudite Emir, the editor, was crossing busy Geary Boulevard in San Francisco, when one of the city's famous blasts of wind yanked the papers from her grip and deposited them on the street in front of the oncoming traffic. She watched in horror as many weeks of writing, editing, typing, correcting, proofreading, and more correcting lay under the wheels of the passing cars. Once the traffic had passed, she rushed out to collect the pages. Luckily, all the tire marks had landed on the wrong side of the sheets, and she was able to retrieve almost every one of the ready-for-printer pages.

Mananam staff in the initial years, planning an issue. (L to R) Rudite Emir (editor), Ruth Lundgren (artist), Byron Hayes (production) ▼

The staff reviewing ▶ Mananam *paste-up at Family Press, Napa, California, in the early years*

In the early days, *Mananam* served as a forum for the Mission's own members to express their understanding of Vedānta. Besides the articles, there were special features such as one-page reflections on chosen verses, explanations of Vedāntic terms, and interviews with Chinmaya Mission workers. There was a news section also, which was dropped when a separate North American newsletter, *CMW News*, began to be published. *Mananam* also featured a children's section and a regular Sanskrit lesson and glossary of Sanskrit terms in each issue. Book reviews and questions–answers were included in some issues. A talented artist, Ruth Lundgren, created original drawings for every issue.

After the first few introductory issues, the focus of the journal shifted to specific themes, such as Guru, temples, and the life and teachings of Ramana Maharshi. Ten issues included a series of self-study lessons on the basics of Vedānta. Later, this series of lessons was published in book form, as also *Mananam*'s series of Vedāntic term definitions.

"The challenges of bringing out these issues were many, but the sādhanā was incomparable," recalls Rudite. "Spending many hours reading spiritual material and challenging oneself to squeeze all critical points of a given theme into a single page of the editorial were hours spent in fulfilling contemplation. I personally also found great fulfillment in being able to collaborate with so many fine writers and associates who helped make *Mananam* what it is."

In 1985, *Mananam* moved to its next phase and the format changed from a journal to a publication series that resembled a book. In a smooth transition, Vilasini Balakrishnan took over the editorial responsibility from Rudite. Vilasini had been accompanying Gurudev as his secretary in his travels all over India between 1981 and 1984. Then Gurudev instructed her to move to the Bay Area of California and relieve Rudite so that she could devote her attention to her growing family. After long discussions, Vilasini and Rudite decided on the change in format, so that *Mananam* would not be time-sensitive as a magazine, but would be cherished as a series of books in the years to come. Gurudev was a little skeptical in the beginning, but when he received the first issue in the new format, he enthusiastically penned back a note to the *Mananam* staff: *"The Choice is Yours: Ethics in Vedānta* has reached me. Something brilliant. Vilasini's idea, when she expressed [it], I did not get a full picture. She has scored. This is a glorious idea." And he immediately instructed Central Chinmaya Mission Trust to reprint 5,000 copies for sale in India. CCMT reprinted all the early issues, and they sold well throughout India.

The focus was now fully on unfolding a chosen theme from Gurudev's writings on Vedānta, and supplementing it with other Mission authors and complementary articles drawn from diverse spiritual traditions. As the opening page states, *"Mananam Publication Series* is dedicated to the exposition of Vedāntic thought, with an emphasis on the unity of all religions." Gurudev would provide themes for issues, and the editors would comb first through Gurudev's writings, then through that of other Ācāryas of the Mission, and finally through other spiritual literature, until a cohesive book took shape. The editor recalls the excitement of discovery, as she and the editorial staff would go through book after book, extracting only the articles that touched the spirit.

Rudite mentored Vilasini through the painstaking process of editing and publishing. Together they selected the leaf logo, which still holds a prominence in every book, including the special Chinmaya Birth Centenary Celebration Series, to which this book belongs. "The leaf," explains Vilasini, "represents the *patra* (leaf) referred to by Śrī Kṛṣṇa in *Bhagavad-gītā* IX:26, when He said: He who with devotion offers Me a leaf, a flower, a fruit, or water, that devout offering I accept."

Mananam remains a humble offering to Pūjya Gurudev, helping to spread Gurudev's precious message around the globe.

Mananam went through a challenging period in 1985 when Vilasini relocated to Cincinnati, Ohio. She left behind, in Los Altos, California, a well-seasoned and inspired staff, including Indra Advani, Uma Jeyarasasingam, John Haring, Nalini and Bill Browning, and, of course, Rudite Emir. After Vilasini started a Chinmaya Study Group and Bala Vihar in Cincinnati, a few Mission devotees came forward to help with the new publication. From concept to article selection and obtaining copyright permissions, from typesetting to manually pasting up the pages, from inserting the diacritical marks to negotiating with a new printer, from stuffing large brown mail bags with zip-sorted batches of envelopes to carrying the books to the post office, the new group shouldered all the responsibilities of bringing out the quarterly publication.

In 1986, *Mananam* made another move with Vilasini to Washington, D.C., where Brni. Arpita (now Swamini Radhikananda), Nancy Patchen, Suresh Balakrishnan, and Veronica Hausman were added to the staff, before it settled in 1988 into its present home in Toronto, Canada, under the able and tireless leadership of Margaret Leuverink (now Dukes). When Gurudev first proposed the idea of editorship to Margaret, she was awe-struck and thrilled. She recalls, "My immediate response was that I would

▲ *Margaret Leuverink (seated) and Rudite Emir during the 4th International Camp in Maryland, 1991*

not be able to handle it, as I was not qualified. But Gurudev lovingly assured me that, with Vilasini's help for a couple of years, I would eventually catch on. Throughout the years, I have realized what a great gift he gave me for the opportunity to study and reflect!" Margaret assembled an inspired team, drawing upon Mission members in Toronto and elsewhere. In 1989, Hazel and David Dukes, who had met Gurudev in Washington, D.C., were added to the editorial staff, providing key typesetting and layout expertise, until, for reason of Hazel's health, they left the team in 1998. Before that, in 1997, it was decided that *Mananam* would be published twice yearly.

For many years, Swami Shantananda has been a mentor and a source of inspiration and encouragement to the *Mananam* team. Among the many volunteers who helped out with precious contributions at various times are Mai Musta, Kumkum Bhatia, and, in particular, Roger Warren (Br. Rajeshwar). He handled the various production jobs for many years, and, after completing the Vedānta Course at Sandeepany, he rejoined *Mananam* as coeditor in Toronto. After he left, other people volunteered, for this was the Lord's work and He would provide!

In 1998, Neena Dev of Toronto joined the team as an associate editor. Her aesthetic touch and creative mind produced many inspiring themes and titles, such as *At Home in the Universe* and *Maya: The Divine Power*. Soon thereafter, the husband and wife team of Arun and Rashmi Mehrotra of Chicago volunteered their services, taking care of all the production duties and assisting with editorial duties as well.

Through the years, various people, including Pat Loganathan, at that time in Buffalo, New York, Vinni Soni in Toronto, and Lynne Matous in Florida, have acted as on-demand assistant editors. In 2004, David Dukes rejoined the team, once again providing his valuable editing and computer skills. In 2009, Padmashree Rao in Houston, Texas, joined, enriching the team with her much-appreciated editing skills and knowledge of the Sanskrit language.

In 2008, Pūjya Guruji, Swami Tejomayananda, asked the *Mananam* team to work on a project that would celebrate Pūjya Gurudev's birth centenary in 2016. He suggested that from 2011 to 2016, the *Mananam* publication shift its focus entirely to a series of twelve books that would herald the centenary celebrations. Each book was to be woven around topics dear to Gurudev's heart, such as spirituality, education, youth, children, family, service, publications, seniors, and so on. Guruji then assigned most of the books to certain Ācāryas and senior sevikās to form their own teams and research and write each book. The *Mananam* team would edit the material and also do the book layout if requested. The second book, titled *Vedānta: Swami Chinmayananda, His Words, His Legacy,* was brought out entirely by the *Mananam* team, and Rudite once again joined the editing team to lend invaluable support.

In 2012, Br. Eric in New Jersey and Aarthi Ramalingam in Chicago joined the team to add their editing skills. Each of the team members brings a unique capability to the publication. Together, they provide powerful clarity and force to the *Mananam* publication.

After 2016, *Mananam* is slated to undergo yet another trans-formation. In a recent meeting with Guruji, he gave the following guidance for future *Mananams*: publish articles that speak philosophically to today's generation and in each issue also include short, to-the-point bits of advice about dealing with situations discussed in the philosophical articles.

Mananam was founded with the intention of assisting Swami Chinmayananda's students of Vedānta, as well as interested readers around the world, with 'a method of inquiry, using the revelations enshrined in the Upaniṣads and other texts of ancient India.' The process of reflection (manana) is the sublime sādhana that follows the process of listening (śravaṇa) to the teachings of the enlightened masters and highly evolved seekers. *Mananam* thus serves as a diving-off point for meditation (nididhyāsana) upon the pure Self. This was

Gurudev's intention when he launched the publication more than thirty-five years ago, and this remains the publication's guiding light.

The titles in the present celebratory centenary series, of which this book is one, also form a take-off point for reflection on the many facets of Pūjya Gurudev and his work. Why did he do what he did? What was the vision behind it? How could one individual expand thus and reach out to many thousands of people? Is this what is meant when the scriptures say that the Lord has thousands of hands and heads? As we contemplate on the Guru who taught us the art of lifting ourselves to the highest plane, we take wings toward the goal he indicates.

Regional Newsletters in India

Besides the main magazines, which have an international circulation, there are many regional newsletters and magazines that fulfill the need for communication within the local populace, some of them in the language of the region. Some are full-fledged magazines, while others are small news bulletins. Of late, some Mission centers have been experimenting with online news bulletins in order to avoid the processing and expense involved in printing and mailing. Some, like the *Chinmaya Dindimah*, published in Chennai, have scaled down from a magazine to a small news bulletin that serves the purpose locally.

Chinmaya Chandrika is the regional magazine in Hindi, brought out from Kanpur, and the origin of this has already been given in detail under the section on the regional publications in Hindi.

The *New Delhi News Bulletin* was started in 1975 by Swami Jyotirmayananda, who was also its first editor. Smt. Anjali Singh served as editor for ten years during different periods. She also printed the magazine at her family printing press. Smt. Bharati Sukhatankar also served as an editor for four years from 1980 to 1984. Miss Anju Virmani, Smt. Shobha Juneja, Dr. Raghunath, Smt. Bhanumati Rao, Smt. Madhu Bawa, and Smt. Gayatri Balasubramaniam were among

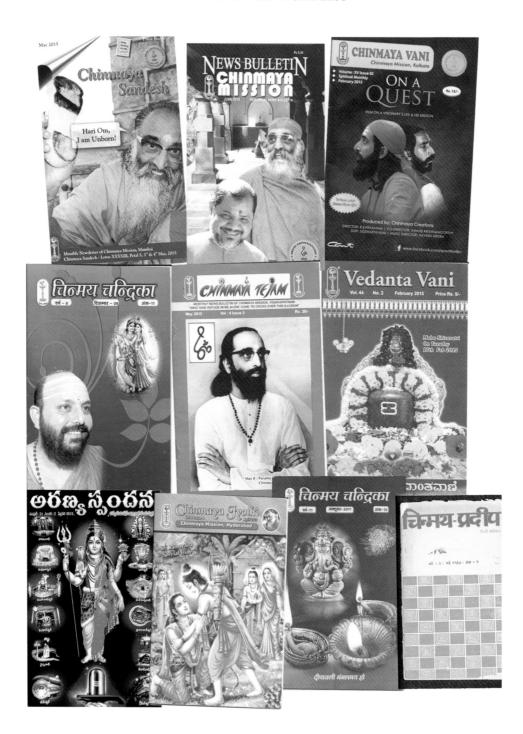

others who offered editorial support. In March 1997, Smt. Indu Shrikent took charge and continues to be the editor to date. Pūjya Gurudev had remarked once that this was one of the best magazines of Chinmaya Mission.

Vedanta Vani is another important magazine, produced by Chinmaya Mission, Bengaluru, for circulation all over the Karnataka region. It is bilingual, with an English section, followed by the Kannada section. Under the guidance of Swami Brahmananda, the magazine carries interesting articles and has served the region for more than forty-two years.

Chinmaya Sandesh is a local magazine in English, published from Mumbai since 1972. It has the advantage of being brought out from the city which houses the headquarters of the Chinmaya Mission. Hence, it often has access to and carries interesting articles, satsaṅgas, and question–answers by Ācāryas in Mumbai, as well as those visiting the Sandeepany Sadhanalaya in Powai. Of late, a greater part of this magazine is devoted to announcements of upcoming events and grassroots activities, reflecting the vibrant growth of the Mission centers in the region.

Chinmaya Vani from Kolkata and *Chinmaya Maauli* from Pune, both in English, have blossomed into full-fledged magazines in the recent years. The old issues of *Tapovan Prasad* carry advertisements for *Chinmaya Pradeep*, the Hindi monthly of

THE ORGAN OF THE CHINMAYA MISSION

"Chinmaya Pradeep" will be thus dedicated in giving the necessary cultural tone to our society. It will not be a mere translation of my works nor will it be only a Hindi-organ to popularise the news of the Mission. This will be an independent organ opening its pages for all creative pen in the world of Hindi literature. Keeping the great immortal Vedantic philosophy as our guiding pole-star we shall be publishing thoughts of the great thinkers of the country which will give the nation a "plan" to live harmoniously an integrated life of national pride and social self-Satisfaction. I congratulate the Editor and his collegues who have decided to take up this work and I am sure that Mother Sruiti will guide their endeavour and bless the generations.

चिन्मय-प्रदीप
हिन्दी मासिक

" CHINMAYA - PRADEEP "
Published on 16th of Every Month
Life Subscription for
De-lux edition Rs. 200/-
Ordinary edition Rs. 100/-
Annual Subscription :
Superior quality paper : Rs. 10/-
Ordinary paper : Rs. 5/-
Single copy : 50 Ps.
PLEASE SEND
YOUR "ARTICLES" AND SUBSCRIPTIONS
TO
Editor :
"CHINMAYA - PRADEEP"
Central Chinmaya Mission Trust.
Band Box House,
254-D, Dr. Annie Besant Road,
Worli, Bombay-18 (W.B.)
Phone : 451331-32.

▲ *Announcement published in* Tapovan Prasad, *June 1965*

Chinmaya Mission, and of *Prama*, a quarterly journal brought out from Ahmedabad, but they no longer exist. Gurudev's inaugural message sent to *Chinmaya Pradeep* was published in the June 1965 issue of *Tapovan Prasad*.

Chinmaya Jyothi from Tripunithura, born twenty-seven years ago, is a Malayalam magazine, but carries a few lead articles in English. *Chinmaya Amrit* is brought out regularly from Amritsar. *Aranya Spandana* has been published in Telugu from 1984 onward by the Chinmayaranyam Publication Trust. There are many other regional magazines in the ever-expanding spectrum of Chinmaya Mission in India. *Chinmaya Drishti* is a biannual publication that keeps all the Chinmaya Vidyalayas not only in touch with each other, but also with the vision of Chinmaya Mission.

Newsletters around the World

CMW News has kept the network of Mission centers and devotees in the U.S. actively interconnected for more than three decades. The first printed precursor of the newsletter was a section in the early editions of *Mananam* when it was being published in magazine format. The newsletter section in the quarterly journal was called *Mananam Newsletter* and contained highlights from Gurudev's lecture tours and his schedule.

Later, the newsletter gained its own separate status and was at first published as a separate short publication, but still titled *Mananam Newsletter* (1979). By 1981, it had metamorphosed into the *Chinmaya Mission West Newsletter*, with an editorial staff headed by Nalini Browning, and various Mission members contributing to the effort, including Uma Jeyarasasingam, Renu Prasad, Barbara Carter, Rajendra Shah, and Sheela Mohan. In the late 1980s, the newsletter was renamed simply *CMW News* and was put on a course of regular monthly publication with Nalini Browning and Rudite Emir at the helm, and with Maurelle Godoy (now Godoy Wyeth) acting as Assistant Editor, and Sharmila Lodhia as the Youth and Children's Editor. Bill Browning of Family Press was the printer, as he had been for many years.

In 1993, the editorial duties were assumed by Brni. Aparna Chaitanya (now Swamini Akhilananda). The bimonthly print version has now yielded place to the electronic version available for free download.

The Voice of Chinmaya from Sri Lanka continues to be a colorful magazine, edited by Smt. Sivanandini Duraiswamy. *Chinmaya Jyoti* from Australia, *Chinmaya Vision* from New Zealand, *Chinmayam* from the U.K., and *Chinmaya Doot* from Flint, MI, U.S.A., are some of the other newsletters published 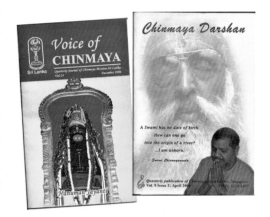 abroad. There are electronic newsletters shared locally in many Mission centers of the U.S. — *Chinmaya Smriti* of Chinmaya Mission Washington Regional Center (CMWRC), *Chinmaya Patrika* of Los Angeles (L.A.), and so on.

Lesson Course

Gurudev's lectures kindled the aspirations of seekers to learn and assimilate more thoroughly the knowledge to which they had been introduced. Since there were not enough sevaks to fulfill these needs abroad, Gurudev found a way out by creating the Postal Lesson Course in 1966. Initially, it was open only to students overseas. Those who passed with honors were acknowledged in the *Tapovan Prasad* magazine.

This systematic scheme of study was much sought after not only by seekers abroad but also by the office bearers in Mission centers, by Study Group members and Bala Vihar sevaks who wanted a better grounding in the scriptures and greater clarity, which would enable them to serve better. Hence, in 1967, the Lesson Course was made available to them. Because of the lack of enough examiners and faculty at Sandeepany Sadhanalaya, the course was not open to the general public, in spite of the great demand for it. Soon the office was shifted from the Mumbai āśrama and placed under the care of Śrī Hamir K. Vissanji.

During the early years, Gurudev himself used to answer the doubts of the students through letters. Gradually, when more sevaks joined the team, the course became available to all members of Chinmaya Mission.

In the early seventies, Pūjya Gurudev had instructed Jorge-Luis Jauregui to conduct Study Groups in English and Spanish for people who had subscribed to the Chinmaya Lesson Course from the San Francisco Bay Area. By 1973, Jorge-Luis had translated the Lesson Course material into Spanish, his native language.

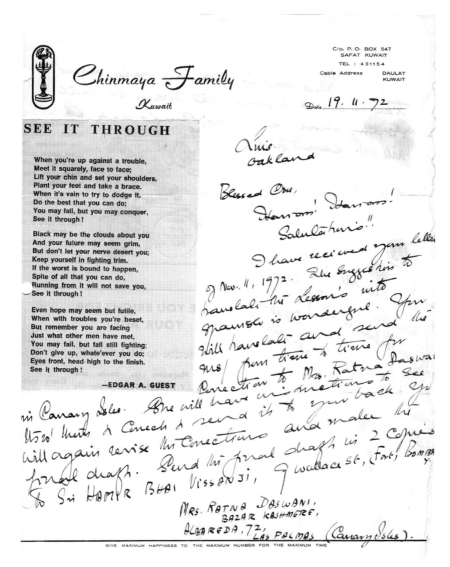

I have received your letter of November 11, 1972. The suggestions to translate the lessons into Spanish is wonderful. You will translate and send the manuscript from time to time for correction to Mrs. Ratna Daswani in Canary Isles. She will have instructions to see through them and correct and send it to you back. You will again revise the corrections and make the final draft. Send the final draft in two copies to Sri Hamir Bhai Vissanji, 9 Wallace Street, Fort, Bombay.

◄ Pūjya Gurudev at the Golden Gate Park, San Francisco, to deliver a talk on U.S. Independence Day, July 4, in the mid-Seventies. (L to R) Byron (a dedicated student of Vedānta), Pūjya Gurudev, David Price (son of Nalini Browning and member of Chinmaya Mission West), Jorge-Luis Jauregui, and Bill Browning, carrying his daughter Anjali

After almost three decades of service, Hamirbhai Vissanji handed the baton to Brni. Vividisha Chaitanya (now Swamini Aaradhanananda). From 1993 to 1996, she was in charge of the Lesson Course, which consisted of twenty-four lessons, handling all the aspects — dispatching lessons and question papers, correcting the answers, maintaining the registers, issuing certificates, and performing other administrative tasks. After her, Br. Varada Chaitanya continued the work. Br. Sagar Chaitanya took charge of the Lesson Course on its last lap at the Sandeepany Sadhanalaya, Mumbai, before moving to Veliyanad, in Kerala.

In the year 2003, the Lesson Course shifted base to Chinmaya International Foundation, Veliyanad. Soon the Foundation Vedānta Course was offered online and there has been no looking back. A whole crop of new Home Study Courses have been introduced, details of which are available in the book *Unto Research* (pages 189–200) in this Mananam Celebration Series, or on the website www.chinfo.org.

PART FIVE

NEW OFFSHOOTS

New Offshoots

Chinmaya Prakashan

Around the year 2006, Manisha Khemlani took charge of the publication division in Mumbai. Slowly, the layout, the look, and the feel of the reprinted books began to change. With advancing technology, more options were available. Books were presented in formats more colorful and attractive than before. Then, Śrī K. C. Patnaik's efforts to place books in commercial bookshops opened up a new trend. Since many of the shops refused to stock books priced below ₹100, it became imperative to publish deluxe editions of some of the books in order to reach new readers. After all, the goal of the publications, as visualized by Pūjya Gurudev Swami Chinmayananda, was to spread the message of the scriptures far and wide.

◄ *Śrī Narain Bhatia, CEO, CCMT, seated on the left, is in serious discussion with (L to R) Śrī Debashish Mohapatra (Financial Controller, CCMT), Manisha Khemlani (COO, CCMT), and Śrī Mahesh Tripathi.*

The new revised editions of old titles incorporated diacritical marks for the English transliteration of Sanskrit words. The publishing approach became more professional. Many more new books were published as we entered the twenty-first century.

Swamini Vimalananda worked hard to bring out the talks of Swami Tejomayananda in book form. A lot of people collaborated to transcribe, edit, typeset, and design the books. Currently, Guruji's prolific compositions in Sanskrit are a category by themselves. The classic quartet of books *Manaḥ Śodhanam*, *Bhakti Sudhā*, *Jñāna Sāra*, and *Dhyāna Svarūpam* present Vedānta in a nutshell. *Ādarśa Jīvan* (*Life of Vision*) presents a collection of songs in Sanskrit, composed for special occasions like birthdays, wedding anniversaries, New Year celebrations, and so on. *Mānasa Bhakti Sūtra*, which gives the essence of *Rāmacaritmānas*, and *Jīvan Sūtrāṇi* (*Tips for Happy Living*), which offers tips and guidelines to live a fulfilling and joyous life, are other examples of his versatile creativity. *Svara to Īśvara* is a unique book on music and spirituality. That book is based on his talk given to Chinmaya Naada Bindu, the music wing of Chinmaya Mission, located in Chinmaya Vibhooti, Kolwan, near Pune.

Apart from the Guru Paramparā's published works on spirituality, the publications wing has expanded to include other genres of books. With the changing times, the Ācāryas of Chinmaya Mission worldwide have had to address many social issues as well. Besides the core teaching of Vedānta, they give talks on parenting, conduct workshops for young couples, and hold camps for senior citizens on the art of graceful aging. The corporate world is ever thirsty for management seminars that blend spirituality and secular success. Consequently, a new crop of books on these topics have been published. Some of the titles in this category are: *Marriage: A Melody, Parenting, You Can, Pathways to Peace, Undoing: Returning to Simplicity, Right Thinking, Conscious Living,* and *Graceful Aging.*

Why Do We

The small book *Why Do We*, authored jointly by Swamini Vimalananda and Smt. Radhika Krishnakumar, has set a record of sorts with the highest sales all over India and abroad. It answers basic questions that often go unanswered by adults because of general ignorance: Why do we wear a bindi? Why do we do namaste? Why do we ring the bell in a temple? The response has been amazing. Orders poured in from abroad, too. To date, more than two lakh (200,000) copies have been sold.

Devotees from Singapore took the lead in bringing out books by Swami Swaroopananda. *Sankaṭa Mocan (Shri Hanuman Ashtakam)*, *Mahā Mṛtyuñjaya (Insights and Inspirations)*, and *Ika Oṅkāra (Meditations on the One Indivisible Truth)* are very popular among a wide variety of readers. *Journey into Health* is an aesthetically designed book and carries a universal appeal.

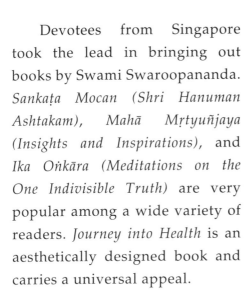

▲ Staff of Chinmaya Prakashan, Mumbai

Smt. Subhashree Raghav (Deputy General ▶ Manager) and Śrī K. C. Patnaik (General Manager) of Chinmaya Prakashan

Pūjya Guruji signs books for Shibani Khorana and other readers at the book stall ▼ (February 16, 2014)

Pūjya Guruji inspects the books on display during the Śivarātri celebrations in Sandeepany Sadhanalaya (February 17, 2015) ▼

With the publications department growing in leaps and bounds, the time was right to build a brand name. In 2013, Pūjya Swami Tejomayananda christened the publications division with the new and distinctive name 'Chinmaya Prakashan.' As of 2015, Chinmaya Prakashan offers almost one thousand titles in various languages. Some of the latest books released are accompanied by CDs with the chanting of mantras, songs sung in specific tunes, or other relevant material.

Collaborations and partnerships with retailers, publishing houses, and distribution centers like Crossword, Oxford, Landmark, and Jaico in India have been developed to further promote published material.

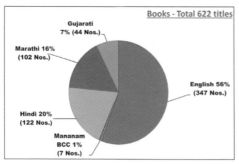

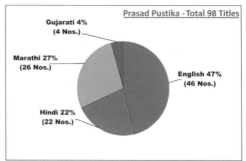

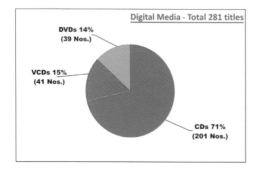

In order to accommodate new reading habits, Chinmaya Prakashan offers a large range of digital media content in CD, MP3, VCD, and DVD formats, and has a wide online platform.

Chinmaya Kalpanam

The new generation of books needed good design and layout. However valuable the thought content they held, they needed to be dressed up attractively to catch the attention of readers. Reprints of the older books, even the commentaries on the Upaniṣads, needed creative design and layout. Initially, the work was outsourced. Later, Yuva Veer Tripti, who was posted in Mumbai, and Shamika Rajesh Shet, who joined as a professional designer, formed the nucleus for the design team. The design team has now grown to a vibrant group of seven people. Pūjya Guruji has given the team the name 'Chinmaya Kalpanam.'

The design team takes care of not only the books but also the publicity material for Chinmaya Mission, such as booklets, pamphlets, and the like.

▲ *The design team at work in Sandeepany Sadhanalaya, Mumbai*

Chinmaya Vani

At the time of this writing, almost every Mission center has its own permanent bookstore. Whenever big book exhibitions are held, especially in major Indian cities, the local Mission center's bookstore takes part actively, and sales often run into lakhs (100,000s) of rupees. These bookstores order books in bulk from Chinmaya Publications to meet the demand during jñāna yajñas in their city. In order to give an identity to these book stalls, Pūjya Swami Tejomayananda named them 'Chinmaya Vani.' These retail bookstores have become vibrant focal points in the Mission centers, drawing the young and old alike.

◄ Chinmaya Vani in Chinmaya Vibhooti, Kolwan, Maharashtra, India

Śrī Kumar Nair at the ▶ Chinmaya Vani bookstore in Mumbai. He has worked there for the last seventeen years.

Chinmaya Mission Chennai has ventured into the bookmobile arena, taking the books to central locations, literally carrying the books to the doorsteps of the readers. This Mobile Chinmaya Vani was the idea of Swami Mitrananda, the dynamic and innovative Ācārya based in Chennai. It has been extremely successful and book sales in and around that city have soared since its inception.

Chinmaya Creations

Chinmaya Creations is the creative visual media wing of Chinmaya Mission. Its biggest project *Upanishad Ganga*, a TV serial with fifty-two episodes, directed by Chandraprakash Dwivedi, was aired weekly with tremendous success on Doordarshan, India's national television channel from March 2012 onward. The well-known Indian actor, Abhimanyu Singh, has played thirty-three different lead roles in this television serial. This project has made an effort to communicate the message of the Upaniṣads through life stories and experiences. 'Vedic

Culture' is introduced in the initial episodes (1–4). Cultural values for the individual and the society are presented in the following eighteen episodes (5–22). Then, after establishing the cultural basis and ethos, the core wisdom of the Upaniṣads is presented in the next twenty episodes (23–42). Practical steps that can help to live this wisdom in one's life are then elaborated in the next nine episodes (43–51). The last episode is a tribute — an expression of gratitude for the Vedic wisdom, which has made

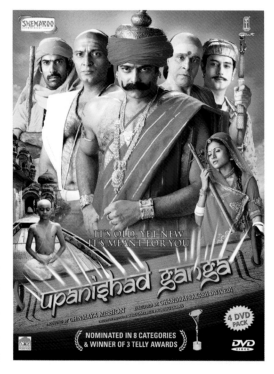

India proud and earned admiration the world over.

Another brilliant production of Chinmaya Creations is *On a Quest*, a two-hour feature film on the life and work of Pūjya Gurudev Swami Chinmayananda. Swami Mitrananda was the brain behind the film and wrote the script, assisted by Yuva Veers. A whole lot of people — Ācāryas, devotees, and members of various wings of the Mission, especially the members of Chinmaya Yuva Kendra — came together to lend their support by taking on one of the acting roles or working behind the scenes. There was great enthusiasm among devotees around the globe to be a part of this project, and they spontaneously came forward to sponsor this film, which was specially created to celebrate Pūjya Gurudev's birth centenary. It was released in Chennai on December 15, 2014, and was received with accolades in theaters all over India and abroad in early 2015.

▲ *A still from the film showing the young Swami Chinmayananda in a contemplative mood near Uttarakasi*

Swami Mitrananda summed up his experience of making the movie:

The statement "You are not the doer" was re-established many a time during the shooting of this film. This was even more evident when people like Sandeep, who played the young Gurudev, Thota Tharani, who played the older Gurudev, and Rajiv, who played Swami Sivananda, came onto the picture exactly when we needed them. Most of these actors not only had a close resemblance to the characters they played, but also came from a Vedāntic background, making it easy to convey the purpose and vision behind this movie.

▲ *Swami Mitrananda in consultation with Śrī Thota Tharani, the famous art director and production designer, who acted the part of the older Gurudev.*

Indeed, things fell into place one after another in miraculous

▲ *A scene where Swami Chinmayananda approaches Swami Tapovan Maharaj with a letter from Swami Sivananda. The role of Swami Tapovan Maharaj (seated with his disciples) was enacted by Karthikeyan, who is Swami Tapovanam's grand nephew.*

ways, and divine Grace could be seen at work every step of the way. The actual shooting of the film was completed in twenty-seven days. The work on the film was a transforming experience for all who participated in it. And this was appropriate, for it was the story of Gurudev, who transformed the lives of thousands of people all through his life.

Chinmaya Vishwasutra

Chinmaya Vishwasutra, also known as Chinmaya Connect, is the information technology wing of Chinmaya Mission. It spearheads the Chinmaya movement on all electronic platforms and serves the growing IT and networking needs of the Chinmaya family worldwide.

It all began in March 2009 with the webcast of *Navāhna Pārāyaṇam* by Pūjya Guruji Swami Tejomayananda on the Internet. It was done in a very primitive way, with a very limited bandwidth, using a basic computer. Later, in October 2009, CCMT, with great zeal, began upgrading the existing IT services at Central Chinmaya Mission Trust, in addition to giving the static, data-centric Chinmaya Mission website a facelift. The first server equipment was purchased and the in-house IT team was set up, flagging off the journey into wired and wireless spirituality.

In the last few years, a number of events have been streamed live. Among them were the talks by Pūjya Guruji Swami Tejomayananda on *Bhakta Bhakti Aur Bhagavān, Ātmabodha, Īśāvāsya Upaniṣad, Kaivalyopaniṣad, Praśnopaniṣad,* and *Jīvan-muktānanda Laharī.* Important events like Rudrābhiṣekam at the Jagadeeshwara Temple and the sessions of Pūjya Gurudev's Sevaks Training Camp were also streamed live.

The unflagging enthusiasm and the inspired hard work of Br. Saket Chaitanya have contributed to the success of this department. The team, which began with just two members including him, has grown to comprise twelve full-time members, and is soon poised to expand further. A number of part-time volunteers and donors contribute in their own way from across the globe. The operations are currently in four major areas: IT infrastructure development and support, Core IT projects, IT-enabled services, and IT advisory support.

▲ *Br. Saket Chaitanya (left) with members of the IT team at work*

Chinmaya Connect is currently the IT backbone for all departments functioning at Central Chinmaya Mission Trust, keeping them in pace with the world of technology. Its vision statement is: 'To spread the Vision of Chinmaya Mission, using latest technologies to maximum people in maximum locations through minimization of barriers and creation of new frontiers.'

In keeping with its vision, Chinmaya Connect is also continuously trying to make a foray into various channels for digital content delivery, which is sure to hold a prominent role in the years to come as a primary source of knowledge transfer and information dissemination.

Chinmaya Connect ensures that Chinmaya Mission has a strong presence on social media. This requires 24-hour surveillance and daily updating, which is done by volunteers who form part of the Global IT team of Chinmaya Connect.

Chinmaya Connect has also created a delightful, child-friendly website *www.chinmayakids.org*, rich in content and graphics, to impart to young minds the wisdom of the ancient scriptures. The site has undergone a complete makeover, with the expertise of dedicated animators, designers, and artists of CCMT.

Thus, Chinmaya Connect continues the work that was so dear to Pūjya Gurudev's heart, carrying spiritual knowledge to an ever-increasing number of people all over the world in ever new and innovative ways.

▲ *A screenshot of www.chinmayakids.org*

Global Chinmaya Mission Website

The global Chinmaya Mission website has a centralized database that allows individual centers to have their own sub-sites within the global site and still have the flexibility of individual layouts. Many other Mission websites, such as tapovanprasad.chinmayamission.com and sandeepany.chinmayamission.com, are also being created and supported by Chinmaya Mission IT.

Apart from the global website, there are around seventy websites of Chinmaya Mission. The intent is to gradually integrate most of the existing websites, rendering a one-stop information source for all Mission activities, events, itineraries, centers, and Ācāryas across the globe, thus giving the user a uniform experience with updated content, wherever they are. The website would support social networking, mobile rendering, and full-fledged shopping carts.

On the audio and visual front, chinmayamission.tv enables members to browse and watch a wide collection of video content, including talks and bhajans by Ācāryas of Chinmaya Mission. The site has recently undergone a facelift and has been integrated with the global Chinmaya Mission website.

Chinmaya Channel on YouTube

The Chinmaya Channel on YouTube, started in June 2009, has become a popular source of content delivery throughout the world, as it is easily accessible to one and all. Besides the uploads by various centers across the globe, with the help of the IT team, regular updates are made to the Chinmaya Channel by the video processing team of the Chinmaya Video Dham. Swamini Vimalananda remarks, "When I visited Canada for the first time in 2013, I found that half of the audience had already heard my talks on YouTube and were tuned in!"

Audio and Video Mobile App

One of the new breakthroughs in technology is live streaming on mobile media. Chinmaya Connect is planning to relaunch an App for this shortly. Provided at a very low bandwidth in small units specifically developed for handheld devices, audio-video talks and satsaṅgas are streamed on the mobile phone. Quotes, prayers, bhajans, inspirational short videos, cartoons, and the entire rendering of *The Holy Geeta*, including verses and commentary by Pūjya Gurudev Swami Chinmayananda, shall be available on the mobile phone and other devices to enrich the spiritual quotient of devotees.

E-Books

E-Books are both convenient and ecologically beneficial, and they are rapidly gaining popularity. Hence, Chinmaya Mission is also converting some of the inspiring titles into e-books for iPad and other devices. Some of these are *Kindle Life, At Every Breath a Teaching, I Love*

You, Evergreen Messages, Say Cheese and *Game of Life*. These are available in popular online stores like Apple-iTunes, Amazon, Flipkart, and Infibeam. More books will be available soon on other websites.

Chinmaya Upahār

There has always been a good market for Chinmaya memorabilia among the devotees in Chinmaya Mission. As early as 1973, *Chinmaya Diary* was published by CCMT and became very popular. Gurudev's signature 'Om' is a constant favorite, whether it is on watches, pendants, or other trinkets. Stationery, envelopes, bookmarks, calendars, and greeting cards, carrying crisp quotations, are hot favorites. All these are available in various outlets, which have been named 'Chinmaya Upahār' and are managed by the Chinmaya Ashish Trust.

▲ *The Chinmaya Upahār stall, alongside the Chinmaya Vani, attracts a lot of visitors.*

The 'Om Lamp' is one of the most important items in this section. Swamini Vimalananda says, "This lamp has a special significance in many ways. 'Om' is the name of Brahman. It represents the highest Truth.

▲ *Attractive items on display at Chinmaya Upahār in Chinmaya Vibhooti*

▲ *Chinmaya Upahār showroom in Chinmaya Vibhooti*

And, of course, this Om is also Gurudev's signature and we invoke the Guru's presence by lighting the lamp. The lamp itself is a symbol of the Light of Knowledge." Pūjya Guruji Swami Tejomayananda points out that, unlike an electric light that is simply switched on, a lamp is used to light another lamp, signifying the transfer of knowledge from the teacher to the taught. The artist in Kumbhakonam, who designed the Om Lamp, was so inspired by the concept that he waived his professional charges. Pūjya Guruji has instructed the Chinmaya family to light the Om Lamp on special days like

▲ *The Om Lamp*

Chinmaya Jayanti and Guru Purnima, besides other festive occasions. The lamp is available in many sizes, from the smallest one that can light up a tiny altar to a mega-sized one to decorate the dais.

▲ *Front cover of coffee-table book by Śrī Narain Bhatia*

▲ *Various kinds of rudrākṣa mālās on display*

Rudrākṣa mālās occupy a place of pride in the Ch
outlets. Śrī Narain Bhatia, CEO and Trustee of Ce.
Mission Trust, has done extensive research work on rudrakṣa and th
multitudinous benefits it confers on those who wear it. He brought out
a coffee-table book on rudrākṣa, which earned him a doctorate. From
the expensive ekamukhī rudrākṣa to japa mālās for daily use, a wide
range of rudrākṣas are available in these outlets.

Conclusion

The publications wing of Chinmaya Mission, so dear to Pūjya
Gurudev, has grown into a mighty tree with many branches, yielding
a rich variety of flowers and fruits. It has adapted to the changing
times, always keeping in mind Pūjya Gurudev's goal. The eternal
Knowledge embedded in our scriptures is made available according
to the needs of the people, to suit different contexts and varied levels
of understanding, through printed books and contemporary forms of
digital media. And it will continue to flourish through the ages, for the
vision of a Master unfolds and expands through the infinite vistas of
time.

Glossary

A

avidyā — non-apprehension of the supreme Reality; macrocosmic *avidyā* is called *māyā*.

B

bhakta — one who follows the path of devotion

D

Devanāgarī — the script in which Sanskrit is written

J

jñāna yajña — 'sacrifice of knowledge,' by which man renounces all his ignorance into the fire-of-knowledge kindled by Him and in Him (*Bhagavad-gītā* 4:28)

K

kīrtana — simple songs in praise of God, in which the audience repeats every line after the lead singer

kuṭiyā / kuṭīra — a tiny hut or a small compact residence

L

Lakshminarayan — Lord Viṣṇu, the husband / lord of Lakṣmī, the goddess of wealth

langoti — loin cloth

leela — play, sport, amusement, pastime

M

maha yajña	great, long series of lectures on Vedānta
mahāsamādhi	final samādhi, where a Self-realized master consciously wills to drop his body
mananam	reflection
mastakābhiśekam	the pouring of holy water on an idol so as to drench it from the top of the head, thus energizing it. The water is collected from India's holy rivers and energized with mantras. Symbolically, it represents a person's thought-flow (water), embracing the deity in meditation.
mokṣa	freedom from limitation (bondage); liberation from the endless cycle of births and deaths

N

nididhyāsana	meditation; the flow of like thoughts related to *Brahman*, to the exclusion of all other thoughts

O

Om	sometimes spelled *aum*; sacred syllable that represents the supreme Reality. Repetition of the syllable combined with meditation on its meaning is considered an effective spiritual practice.

P

pādukās	olden-time Indian footwear consisting of a sole and a knob that is gripped by the big and second toes; used even today by austere sādhus

prachar	preaching, dissemination, promulgation
pra da pus a	booklet distributed at the end of a jñā-yajña in the form of a blessing; generally given after the Guru-dakṣiṇā is offered by the devotee
Purana	'ancient'; any one of the eighteen books of stories, attributed to Vyāsa, in which Vedāntic ideas are objectified and dramatized in the lives of saints, kings, devotees, and divine incarnations

R

roṭī	flat and round wheat bread, like a pancake

S

sannyāsa	formal renunciation
sannyāsa dīkṣā	formal process of permission and initiation of a seeker into sannyāsa, by the Guru
śiṣya	student; disciple
śloka	verse
śravaṇam	devoting the ears to the hearing of spiritual knowledge; a prescribed spiritual practice/process

V

vānaprastha	the third stage of life wherein one retires from worldly duties — the other stages being brahmacarya (first stage), gṛhastha (second stage), and sannyāsa (fourth stage)

nborn dispositi
deep in the unconscious
formed in the personality when one
the world with egocentric desires

vibhūti

the sacred ash left behind by the special
wood that is burned during a fire worship,
or homa; considered holy and placed on the
forehead as a blessing

Y

yajñaśālā

place where yajña is performed

...ri characters are tran...erate... according... e sch... opted by the International Congress of Orientalists... Athens in 1912. In it one fixed pronunciation value is given to each letter; f, q, w, x, and z are not called to use. An audio recording of this guide is available at www.chinmayamission.com/scriptures.php. According to this scheme:

	sounds like		*sounds like*
a	o in son	ṇ	n in under*
ā	a in father	t	t in table
i	i in different	th	th in thumb
ī	ee in feel	d	th in this
u	u in full	dh	dh in Gandhi
ū	oo in boot	n	n in nose
ṛ	rh in rhytham*	p	p in pen
ṝ	**	ph	ph in phantom*
ḷ	**	b	b in boil
e	e in evade	bh	bh in abhor
ai	i in core	m	m in mind
au	o in now	y	y in yes
k	c in calm	r	r in right
kh	kh in khan	L	L in love
g	g in gate	v	v in very
gh	gh in ghost	ś	sh in shut
ṅ	an in ankle*	ṣ	s in sugar
c	ch in chuckle	s	s in simple
ch	ch in witch*	h	h in happy
j	j in justice	ṁ	m in improvise
jh	jh in jhansi	ḥ	**
ṣ	ny in banyan	kṣ	tio in action
ṭ	t in tank	tr	th in three*
ṭh	**	jṣ	gn in gnosis
ḍ	d in dog	`	silent 'a'
ḍh	dh in adhesive		

* These letters don't have an exact English equivalent. An approximation is given here.

** These sounds cannot be approximated in English words.

Patrons and Contributors

Grateful acknowledgements and special thanks to the following:

DAVID & MARGARET DUKES

| TORONTO, ONTARIO, CANADA |

TAPOVAN PRASAD

| CHENNAI |